THIS book is an attempt to introduce the ordinary reader to the effort of the Western mind, sustained for centuries, to grapple with the major problems of human life and destiny. For this purpose, two outstanding figures are selected from each of the major periods of European development and their contribution to thought is set out: connecting links are provided so that the story may make something of a whole I have endeavoured throughout to avoid technical language as far as the subject permits and to concentrate on essentials. No previous knowledge is assumed, but only interest. I do not, of course, pretend that no difficulties remain; but the reader who finds Aristotle and Kant no easy country to explore may take heart from the fact that even the experts sometimes confess themselves lost. My advice therefore is to pass over at the first reading any sections that prove reluctant to yield up their meaning and to return to them later for further study.   E. L. ALLEN

FROM PLATO
TO NIETZSCHE

BY E. L. ALLEN

BRITISH TITLE:

GUIDE BOOK TO WESTERN THOUGHT

FAWCETT PREMIER • NEW YORK

A Fawcett Premier Book
Published by Ballantine Books

First printed in Great Britain, 1957 by The English Universities Press Ltd. under the title GUIDE BOOK TO WESTERN THOUGHT.

ISBN 0-449-30040-4

This edition published by arrangement with Association Press

Printed in Canada

First Fawcett Premier Edition: March 1962
First Ballantine Books Edition: December 1983
Seventh Printing: January 1990

CONTENTS

ACKNOWLEDGEMENTS

Acknowledgement is made to the following publishers for permission to quote from the books mentioned: Clarendon Press (Ross: *Selections from Aristotle*); Oxford University Press (Gilby: *Philosophical* and *Theological Texts* from St. Thomas Aquinas); Macmillan & Co. (Norman Kemp Smith's translation of Kant); Sheed & Ward (*The Confessions of St. Augustine,* translation by F. J. Sheed); Penguin Books (Cohen's translation of Rousseau: *Confessions*); United Lutheran Publication House (the Philadelphia edition of Luther's Works).

I am grateful to the colleagues and friends who have read the various chapters of this book and given me the benefit of their criticism and special knowledge. If I do not mention their names, it is so that they may not incur any responsibility for my errors and omissions. I am indebted also to my secretary, Mr. Mitchell, for assistance in typing.

E. L. ALLEN

King's College,

Newcastle-upon-Tyne

To Laura

PART ONE
PLATO

CHAPTER I Socrates

THE discovery that "the unexamined life is not liveable by man" was the beginning of the intellectual adventure of the West, and it was the Greeks who made that discovery. Yet it was more than a discovery: it was a decision for a new kind of life, and a decision that had its counterpart in the foundation of Greek colonies east and west in the Mediterranean Sea. The barbarians, the non-Greek peoples of the time, were content to live by tradition and custom; the Greek doubted, asked questions, wanted reasons. So in the inner world as in the outer he hazarded the voyage.

> Far from the shore, far from the trembling throng
> Whose sails were never to the tempest given.

The Greek dared to believe that self-criticism need not destroy a society, but would give it a cohesion all the stronger because it was the product of consent. In the city laws were not imposed by a monarch; the free people gave laws to themselves. The dialogues of Plato reflect a society in which discussion was accepted as the way to truth, and his own inspiration was derived from that most ruthless of all questioners, Socrates. And we all have learned from these two men that truth is not given to us ready-made but is to be sought at great cost.

To be sure, it would be wrong to write the story of those vigorous days as though every Greek, or at least every Athenian, was as alert and uncompromising as Socrates. The democracy that sentenced him to death had had more examination from him than it was prepared to stand, and the young men who had associated with him were not all exactly models of virtue. The average Athenian was probably fairly accurately represented by Aristophanes, who regretted the good old days when parental authority was respected and the accepted standards were sufficient guides to conduct. But just as Israel is a force among us to this day by reason of its prophets and not of the stiff-necked multitude who stoned them, so our debt to Greece is to the few whose names stand first in that "long line of men of thought from Thales to the present day, men individually powerless, but ultimately the rulers of the world".[1]

The Greek mind was like an instrument sharpened and ready to cut, but with little as yet on which to exercise itself. Hence the brilliance of its achievements in logic and mathematics, as compared with the little it has bequeathed to us in science. The earliest thinkers began by questioning nature, but they had not yet the technique that could force an answer from her. The fifth century produced a set of teachers who were more successful because they turned their attention to man and society, for there observation was enough and did not need to be supplemented by experiment. These we know as the sophists. They belonged to the greater Greece that had arisen in the process of colonization; they were in touch with non-Greek peoples, they had travelled and gained a diversity of experience. They asked whether the standards by which men acted in Athens and Corinth were really as sacred and as integral to human nature as had been thought; were they not perhaps the conventions of particular cities with no sanction outside their borders? It was their function to raise these questions; they were not always able to answer them, and when they offered answers, these did not always agree. So they fell under suspicion of being merely glib talkers who trained others to be the same: they could make the worse reason appear the better; they were specialists in rhetoric who could teach a demagogue to persuade a popular assembly, and they were indifferent to the truth or falsehood of his plea, the justice or injustice of his policy.

How difficult it is for us to say how far this portrait of the sophist is a fair one can be seen from the fact

---

[1] A. N. Whitehead: *Science and the Modern World*, 1927, final sentence.

that Aristophanes regarded Socrates as the typical Sophist, while for Plato he belonged in another class altogether. Who was this Socrates? As you read the *Apology* you find that he refuses to stay in Athens and the past; he steps out of its pages and challenges us today. Which of us would care to be button-holed by an unprepossessing, talkative fellow and addressed in this way:

> You, my friend—a citizen of the great and mighty and wise city of Athens—are you not ashamed of devoting yourself to acquiring the greatest amount of money and honour and reputation, and caring so little about wisdom and truth and the greatest improvement of the soul, which you never regard or heed at all? [2]

We are apt to look for an opportunity to get rid of those who use such language to us. Plato was surely thinking of Socrates when he wrote of the just man who is "reputed altogether unjust, that his justice may be tested as being proof against ill-repute and its consequences", so that he will "go on his way unchanged until death".[3]

Two features in Plato's portrait of Socrates call for special attention. The first is *the use of reason to decide moral questions*. That a man should act in a certain way because that is customary in his society or because he has always done so, can never satisfy his questioning intellect. He insists that men must act rationally, must think and decide for themselves, and must be guided by general principles that will bear close scrutiny. But alongside of this we notice *a sense of mission*. He is the gad-fly God has sent to sting that lumbering beast, the Athenian democracy. He follows an inner light, the divine voice that is always negative in its admonition, bidding him now abstain from politics and now refuse the offer of his friends to get him safely out of the city. This is not some queer streak in him for which the historian of philosophy must apologize: it is a warning given at the outset that a philosophy can only be rightly understood as the effort to give rational form to a vision that is intensely personal.

[2] R. W. Livingstone: *Portrait of Socrates*, 1944, p. 26.
[3] *The Republic of Plato*, trans. A. D. Lindsay, p. 45.

The Theory of Forms (a)

IF now we ask what Plato's vision was, the answer can scarcely be given better than in words originally used in a different, albeit similar connection. It was "the vision of something which stands beyond, behind, and within, the passing flux of immediate things".[4] This quest was at once theoretical and practical, for he had, as we have seen, two groups of predecessors, one interested in nature and the other in man, and he shared both their interests. Our experience presents us at once with change and with permanence; we could not live without variety, but neither could we live without stability. But when we go on to ask which of these two is more fundamental and holds the key to the explanation of the others, there we begin to divide. Among Plato's predecessors one, Heraclitus, opted for change. Everything, he said, is in flux; one cannot even step twice into the same river, because it is not the same now as it was a moment ago. Another, Parmenides, opted for permanence. That which is, just *is*, and change is illusory.

"One path only is left for us to speak of, namely, that *It is*. In this path are very many tokens that what is, is uncreated and indestructible, for it is complete, immovable and without end."[5]

Was it not possible that each of these views contained an element of truth, that we must seek an account of the world that does justice to permanence and change alike? In the same way, Plato fell heir to the relativism of the sophists and to the moral earnestness of Socrates. It was only too clear that the rule of life by what is done in a society had broken down; the sophists were not responsible for that, they had only pointed to what was happening all around them. The average man, once he had begun to think and ask questions, was in a state of confusion; it was easy to tangle

[4] A. N. Whitehead, *Op. Cit.*, p. 238.
[5] Frag. 8 in J. Burnet, *Early Greek Philosophy* (1948), p. 174.

him in self-contradiction and reduce him to despair. That was necessary, no doubt, if ever he was to pass from the morality of custom to that of personal insight and decision; but the mistake of the sophists was that they stopped halfway. Socrates did not; he thought his way through to a clarity and resolution that enabled him to accept death rather than disobey the inward monitor. He wanted to take others with him along the road of fearless discussion, close scrutiny and clear definition of moral concepts; but most found the road too arduous. Plato did not, and he would continue the work of his master.

As has been said already, the Greeks possessed an intellectual power at which we still stand amazed, but not the stored-up material we have on which to exercise it. It is not that we are superior, but that we arrived on the scene so much later. There was one sphere, however, in which the lack of material did not matter, since the intellect could itself supply what was needed. That was the sphere of mathematics, a study to which Plato was greatly attracted. As he saw it, a distinction must be drawn between the triangles, circles, points and so on with which geometry deals and of which Euclid supplies the definitions, and the triangles etc. that we actually encounter in our experience. The latter are rough and imperfect but by way of compensation they can be seen and operated upon; the former are perfect, but the price we have to pay for this is that they are accessible only to thought. They belong as it were in two different worlds. Yet these are not *wholly* different, for the surveyor and the navigator would be sadly at a loss did not the constructions of the mathematician apply to the world in which they do their work. Shall we say the triangle on the ground 'participates in' or 'imitates' the triangle with which the mathematician operates?

A similar conclusion follows when we consider moral concepts. When two men debate whether one path is longer than another, they are only able to do so because there is somewhere a common standard, perhaps a yardstick, perhaps an ordnance survey map, to which to appeal. In the same way, when the question is which of two courses of action would be the more just, it is assumed that somewhere there is a standard of justice to which appeal may be made. But of course this second standard is not as accessible as the first; it is grasped by the mind, not observed by the senses. It is possible indeed to argue that justice is what we decide is in our own interest when we are ourselves in power, and this is the view one of the speakers puts forward in the *Republic*. But it is not satisfactory, for it clearly makes sense to ask whether such a standpoint is just. We seem driven to admit that there is a justice, a humanity, a truth we do not make but find. But where are these things? Not, alas, in this world below, where all our justice is subject to correction by fuller knowledge, all our humanity is sadly limited, and all our truth is infected at some point with error. Again, shall we say that our acts are just because they somehow 'participate in' or 'imitate' the justice we apprehend with the mind?

This is Plato's Theory of Forms, which has fascinated the Western mind since it was first formulated. It is an effort to do justice alike to what is changing in our experience and to what is permanent. To the former we have access by the senses, and all that these yield must be classed as belief or opinion; the mind or intellect is at home with the latter, and it is the realm of knowledge. There are times when a gulf seems to open between these two worlds, so that one is in heaven and the other on earth, one eternal and the other temporal. The writer of the epistle to the Hebrews has employed this scheme to vindicate Christianity as against Judaism; the eternal temple in the heavens reduces the earthly temple to a mere copy and shadow, destined to be destroyed. But Plato was not a mystic who fled this troubled world: he saw active service in the wars of his time, and he was called to Sicily as a political adviser, and, as we shall see, he was intensely interested in some of the most practical problems. Therefore we must never forget that what he saw as eternal stands not only beyond but also "behind and within the passing flux of immediate things". The world of Forms is also the underlying structure of this transitory world.

CHAPTER III   The Theory of Forms (b)

ONE of the earliest criticisms of Plato to come down to
us is that of Aristotle, who accuses him of solving the
problem of how to hold together the changing and the
permanent by separating them into two distinct worlds
and then looking vainly round for some means of
establishing a connexion between them—for Aristotle
dismisses 'participation' as meaningless. There are times
when Plato used language that justifies such a criticism,
and it is certainly in this sense that he was mainly understood in the past. The Platonist was a 'realist' in the
technical sense of that term in the history of philosophy;
one who holds that general ideas such as 'man' and
'horse' are not mere constructions of the mind, they
are means by which we apprehend something real, the
'essence' of horseness, as it were, the ideal or pattern
horse that is more real than the particular horse we know
so that the particular horse has only the reality it
borrows from this essence. It is easy to see what difficult questions this raises. Is there an essence or Form
for every object? Is there one, so Plato's critics asked,
for dirt and hair and evil and everything else we come
across in the world we live in?

One important element in Plato's legacy to the Western world is his conviction—or should we call it
his presupposition?—that the universal ranks higher
than the particular, the horse-in-itself than any of the
horses entered for last week's race, and that truth is
grasped by an effort of the intellect rather than by the
senses. We are inclined to the opposite presupposition.
It may help us to understand Plato better if we recall
that a physicist may be more interested in 'the atom as
such' than in any particular atom; the latter indeed is
for him only a point at which he has access to the former.
But here a major difference enters in. For Plato is sure
that we do not derive our knowledge of the Forms from
observation, leaving out what belongs to a particular
thing and concentrating on what is common to every
instance of that kind of thing. Knowledge of the Forms
is in our minds from the outset, but latent there and

15

needing to be brought out by contact with objects. The triangle we see brings to mind the triangle as such, the absolute and eternal triangle; it is not as if we discovered something new but as if we recollected something we had forgotten.

In the dialogue *Meno* we see Socrates teaching a slave some of the elementary principles of geometry, not by instructing him in them, but by eliciting them from him by means of diagrams. In the process, he is made aware of knowledge he did not suspect himself to possess. Plato offers an explanation of this in the form of a story or myth. According to this, the soul in each person existed before birth, in another world than this, a world inhabited by the gods and by the Forms. There we were familiar with mathematical objects and relations, as also with moral ideals such as "beauty, goodness, justice, holiness": indeed, we must have acquired such knowledge before birth. But alas, we lost at birth all this knowledge, but "afterwards, by the use of the senses we recovered what we previously knew—we previously possessed". If that is so, it follows that "the process which we call learning" is "a recovery of the knowledge which is our own".[6] It is easy to see to what conception of education this leads. The teacher does not fill the empty mind of the child; his instruction is the reagent that brings to light what was once written there by the finger of God.

Does Plato mean us to take this story literally? Or is he simply saying that the human mind has a structure of its own, so that it does not merely take in what observation supplies, but operates on this material to co-ordinate and classify and generalize, though we do this unconsciously until someone comes along who helps us to understand what we are doing? If Plato had written a systematic treatise, he would have told us; as it is, he wrote dialogues, offering suggestions for the reader to consider. That strange dialogue *Parmenides* makes it clear that Plato was aware of the difficulties of his theory, and Aristotle does not spare him in his *Metaphysics*. Yet no refutation of the theory has been able to dispose of it; after more than two thousand years it

[6] Livingstone, *Portrait of Socrates*, 1944, p. 119. Wordsworth's *Ode on the Intimations of Immortality* makes use of Plato at this point. But with him, experience makes us forget, not remember.

fascinates us still. It does so, not because it has solved our problems, but because it provides the best symbolism yet available for one of our most cherished institutions. We are sure that this world with its tangle of justice and injustice is not all there is, and we appeal from it to an ideal of absolute justice we pledge ourselves to serve. Moral ideals belong in a purer atmosphere than we breathe here below; yet, our life can participate in them, resemble them, copy them.

We may abandon Plato's theory of Forms and yet retain the vision that inspired it, the vision of Truth, Beauty, and Justice. Nothing can finally satisfy us but these, for they are absolute and eternal. At one point Plato suggests that the Forms constitute a hierarchy, a pyramid with the Form of the Good at the summit. Probably he does not mean 'good' in the sense of morally good merely, but in the sense of our 'value'. There is a Supreme Value from which all else derives its being and in the light of which all else is to be understood. We may identify this with God; he does not. Elsewhere he bids us aspire beyond all that is beautiful in this world to the final Beauty, which we shall then see "as absolute, existing alone with itself, unique, eternal, and all other beautiful things as partaking of it". To that Beauty no man can attain without intellectual effort; yet it is given to him at the last by revelation.[7] We may have doubts about the language in which Plato describes this pilgrimage to the Absolute; his invitation to the pilgrimage remains.

CHAPTER IV   The Soul

IT is clear that the soul is cast for a role of crucial importance in Plato's thinking. It belongs to both worlds, the higher one of the intellect and the lower one of the senses. This is expressed in story-form by saying that it belonged to the former before birth and entered at birth on the latter. We might also drop the story-form and say that the soul is at once the intellectual power that grasps the eternal Forms and the percep-

[7] *Symposium*, trans. W. Hamilton, 1951, p. 94.

tive activity to which the sense-world is revealed. Being at home in both realms, it is able to judge the things of sense by the Forms. But the word 'soul' had for Plato and the Greeks generally a much wider sense; it stood for the principle of life and motion generally. As has often been pointed out, whereas we assume that a body will be in motion unless prevented by something external to it, the Greeks assumed that a body will be at rest unless motion is imparted to it from outside. Now, the soul is "the motion which can set itself moving",[8] and therefore explanation in terms of it must take precedence of any appeal to mechanical causation. In the end, therefore, Plato came to infer a Soul (World-soul) sustaining the universe, and souls of a lower order responsible for movements that accorded or clashed with the basic pattern of movement.

But it is not this conception of the soul that has been influential, but rather one that appears in the *Republic* and another that serves to supply Socrates in the *Phaedo* with some famous arguments for immortality. We are told in the *Republic* that three parts can be distinguished within the soul. We might prefer to say that the soul functions at three distinct levels; but somehow we have to do justice to the all-too-familiar fact of conflict within the self. The three parts are termed the reasoning, the spirited or assertive, and the desiring.[9] Each of these has its specific 'virtue' or right exercise of function; wisdom, courage, and temperance respectively. But, of course, a man is a total self or at least he should seek to become such, and we therefore need a name for the fourth virtue, which will consist in the right balance between these. That is justice or righteousness. But this fourth virtue comes about as the rational part of the soul brings under its rule the other two parts. As we should say, the integration of the personality comes about as reason establishes control over instinct and emotion.

There is further a difference in value between the spirited and the desiring elements of the soul, for the

[8] *The Laws of Plato,* trans. A. E. Taylor, 1934, p. 287.

[9] An escaped prisoner, after being without food for days, comes across a village. Desire says: "Go and ask for food"; reason, "You will be recaptured"; and there is that in him which may make him take the risk or may make him continue to hold out.

former is more ready to submit to reason than the latter. Incidentally, it is worth considering how far this opinion of Plato's is accurate. Is it not the case that men are led astray just as easily by an appeal to their generous and 'manly' impulses as to their animal appetites and lusts? But Plato has no doubts on the point, and in one of the most beautiful of the myths, in the *Phaedrus,* he describes the soul as a chariot drawn by two horses, one good and one bad, with a charioteer, reason, directing it. The spirited and the desiring parts of the soul now represent two forms of Love, one spiritual and the other sensual, one attracted to the eternal beauty in the beloved and the other to his physical beauty. The figure is complicated by the representation of the soul as winged in its pre-existent state, when it kept company with the gods, and losing its wings at birth, though, especially in the case of the philosopher, they sprout again when he is led to recollect here what he saw there.

The conception of the soul as pre-existent has a religious origin. Plato has it taken over from Orphism, for which the soul was a divine element imprisoned in and hampered by a mortal body. Greek admits of a play on the words body (*sōma*) and tomb (*sēma*). In the Phaedo, where we join the friends of Socrates who keep him company in the last moments of his life, the soul is no longer the principle of life and motion, no longer the scene and combatants of the moral struggle; it is a divine stranger inhabiting this world for a brief period, and yearning for death as the release by which it will return to its true home. One of the theses Socrates maintains is that the soul is clogged and hampered by the body in the exercise of its truest functions, dragged down into the sense-world when it aspires to the Forms. The philosopher is the man who lives most for the soul and least for the body, so that he can be said to anticipate death and to lead here and now a dying life. The soul, it is further argued, is simple and as such is exempt from dissolution; it survives the attack of its worst enemy, evil, and therefore need not fear that of death; it is superior to the body and therefore meant to survive it. The assertion of immortality expands at more than one point into a description of the soul's fate in the after life, the period of discipline and purgation it goes through, and the conditions under which it takes on another life in this world.

No one today is likely to be won over to a belief in immortality by the arguments in the *Phaedo*. We cannot equate the soul with good and the body with evil as readily as is done here; moreover, it is clear that Plato did not always do so. He frequently admits that the soul can be either good or evil according to its choices.

The modern reader will be more at home with the *Apology*. There Socrates recognizes that death is a venture into the unknown, and the guiding thread in our hands as we enter it is not argument but hope. Perhaps death is the end, perhaps it is a meeting with the great and good whose names we have treasured since we heard them first. The true man will be ready for either possibility; which will be actualized, quite literally God only knows.

CHAPTER V   The State

IT has been remarked already that there was a strong practical bent in Plato and that he participated fully in the stirring events of his time. He lived in a society for which politics was an absorbing, and sometimes a cruel passion, and in which the divisions between states were matched and exacerbated by those within states. In the long war between Athens and Sparta, in which both Socrates and he served, the democracies sided with the first and the aristocracies with the second, so that the victory of one party carried with it the exile, if not the massacre of the other. The victory of Sparta therefore led to the suppression of democracy in Athens. But in Plato's eyes the Athenian democracy stood condemned much less for military weakness than for lack of unity; nor could he ever forgive it the condemnation of his master. The *Republic* shows us the theoretical counterpart to that practical political activity in which he and his disciples were always willing to engage.

The state he describes there is, of course, the city; that was the political unit in Greece in his day. What he most desires for such a city-state is unity and harmony, an end to the hideous atrocities of class-war. The city must be one city, not one of the rich at strife with another of the poor within the same walls. Yet unity is not uniformity; the city, like the soul, achieves unity through the recognition of different abilities, each with its function, but all co-operating for the common good. There will therefore be three estates (we must not call them classes, for that would suggest hostility) corresponding to the three aspects of the soul. These will be the wise men, the brave men, and the useful men. Again, as in the soul there is an affinity between reason and courage, so the rulers of the city will be drawn from the military. The guardians and the soldiers—these are the first two estates; we will call the third the producers. Plato's attention is concentrated upon the guardians. As he sees it, the best way to secure a sound state is to train up an élite that will have the common good at heart and as such will be accepted and obeyed by the rest of the population.

So what began as a suggestion in the field of politics develops into a projected system of education. We recognize today that every society needs an élite that will set its standards and give it leadership. We tend to look to the universities to produce such an élite for us. How did Plato propose to obtain one? He makes it clear that they are to be elect for responsibility and not for privilege. Singled out for their high calling by the possession of certain natural aptitudes, they are to be trained as dedicated servants of the common good. Their earlier instruction will be in 'music' and 'gymnastic', or, as we should say in the fine arts and literature, along with physical training. Higher education will be in mathematics and philosophy, that is, the theory of the Forms, and will be continued to the age of thirty-five. Those who have completed the course will then enter the service of the state, retiring at fifty to serve as elder statesmen in an advisory capacity.

Certain features of this system of education evoked criticism at the time, so that it was modified when Plato wrote later in the *Laws* on the same subject. For example, the guardians are to have all things in common, and must not possess wealth of their own. More serious than that, they are not to enjoy home life of any kind, but men and women are to mate under civic control so as to beget the best children, and no child is to know who his parents are, but all are to be wards of the state. Yet the woman is not valued merely as she can beget children; where she possesses the same aptitude as the man, she is to receive the same training and to render the same service. Everything, that is to say, is to be stamped out that would attach a person otherwise than to the community; he must be disinterested in all he does. Further, artist as Plato was (and he is pre-eminent among philosophers for literary skill and dramatic power), the overriding needs of the state made him call for a strict censorship, even of music, on moral grounds. The guardians-to-be must hear no soft, relaxing tunes, but only those that inspire high endeavour and self-control. The stories of Homer and the other poets must be expurgated; indeed, it might be necessary to exclude them outright. For do they not present the gods as engaged in unworthy actions or yielding to weak and base emotions? One simple criterion must be employed: only that which is good may be ascribed to the gods.

The whole scheme is, as Plato avowed, an attempt to solve the standing problem of politics. Political action is not possible save by the exercise in some degree of power by some persons over others. Now, those who want such power are almost certain to abuse it. Power over persons is so dangerous a thing that only those can be trusted with it who do not want it. A disinterested élite alone can supply what is needed. And they will be trained in something more than the techniques of organized society. They must be devoted to the ends that society should serve, not merely experts in the means it employs. That is the purpose of their training in philosophy; they are to see how everything in the world and in the mind of man should be governed by a vision of the Good, of the ultimate Value. But, alas, such men are not wanted in politics; any advice is preferred to that of the man of principle. There is only one inference to be drawn:

Neither city nor constitution . . . will ever be perfect, until fortune grant that some necessity encompass the philosophers, and those few that are not evil, but who are now called useless, so that whether they will or not they take charge of the city, and find the city obedient to them, or until upon those who are now in dominions and kingdoms or upon their sons some breath of heaven send a true love of true philosophy.[10]

CHAPTER VI   Origins

IN our own day, the most influential of all Plato's dialogues is the *Republic*; indeed, it is often the first book to be put in the hands of the adult student who comes new to philosophy. The rise of the totalitarian state has made the *Republic* perhaps less attractive but at the same time of greater contemporary interest. But it has not had the influence on the European mind of another dialogue, one of the latest, apparently, that Plato wrote. This is the *Timæus*, which seemed to the Middle Ages to offer a philosophical version of the Christian doctrine of creation. Modern scholars are more aware of the difference between the two conceptions, however closely the language may at times approximate. A second element in the dialogue made it of special interest for those who carried on Plato's work in the Academy or institute of higher studies founded by him. That was its attempt to find the key to the structure of the world and the character of its contents in numbers and mathematical relationships. It is not possible to touch on this latter aspect here.

The account of the physical universe that the *Timæus* offers can be read in two ways, first as a story and then as a piece of logical analysis. It is the former that has a deceptively theistic ring about it. Thus, the origin of things is found in a being who is described as "the maker and father of this universe", who was motivated solely by the desire to communicate his inherent goodness. "God's desire was that all things should be good, nothing, so far as might be, bad." In the making of the universe, he had at his disposal a material that he simply found available; it was "not at rest, but in discordant and disorderly motion", and he fashioned it according to the eternal Forms as his pattern. So "this

10 *Republic,* p. 218.

our world, a creature with life, soul, and understanding, has verily come to be through the providence of God". [11] All this reads amazingly like Gen. i—till we look more closely into it, when we find that the god of whom Plato speaks is no creator but only a craftsman doing his best with what was at his disposal, termed variously 'the receptacle', 'necessity', 'the errant cause' and even 'space'.

But Plato tells us that we are to regard this account as 'a likely story'. It may be that what he has in mind is an analysis of the universe, the total object of our knowledge and investigation, without suggesting that any one of the three factors he finds in it preceded or caused in any way the other two. As such, his philosophy has come to new life in the thought of A. N. Whitehead. If I examine any phenomenon in the world of nature, say a mountain, I can detect it in two aspects. First, there are those qualities that it has in common with all other mountains and not anything else. Second, there is the sheer brute fact that something actually *is* here and now. The one ensures that if there is to be anything existing, the mountain-pattern is available, as it were to be stamped on it; the second that something is available to take the stamp. But how does the stamp in fact get applied, for that there *are* mountains we know? Recourse must be had to a 'principle of concretion' that determines, not now *what* things may be nor *that* things may be, but what things actually *shall* be. [12]

Perhaps the most memorable sentence in the dialogue is that which affirms that "this universe" was "compacted in the beginning by the victory of reasonable persuasion over necessity". [13] By necessity is meant not, as we might suppose, some rigid system of law. How could that be subject to persuasion? No, Plato has in mind rather what we have called sheer brute fact, what medieval theologians termed 'the contingent' and existentialists like Sartre 'the absurd', that for which no reason can be given but which simply *is*. The victory

[11] Plato: *Timæus and Critias,* trans. A. E. Taylor, 1929, pp. 26f.

[12] This, of course, is not to be taken as an exposition of Whitehead's metaphysics, but merely as an attempt to use his language for the interpretation of the *Timæus.*

[13] *Op, cit.,* p. 46.

of persuasion over necessity—what images it calls up! The myths of the ancient Near East turned often upon the triumph of cosmos over chaos, of Marduk over Tiamat; civilization lives by the subjection of the dark irrational powers within the self to the rule of reason. The Greek was aware of a turmoil within himself that threatened him even more than the barbarian beyond his gates; he hoped, in this case at least, that he could win the victory over it by persuasion. The Christian doctrine of creation would stand to gain could it incorporate this insight that the world came about by no display of power but by winning the consent of freedom.[14]

For further reading:

Translations as cited in the text.
A. E. Taylor: *Plato: the Man and his Work. Socrates.*
J. L. Stocks: *Plato and Aristotle.*
G. C. Field: *Plato and his Contemporaries. Plato.*

[14] So Nicolas Berdyaev: *The Meaning of the Creative Act,* 1955.

PART TWO

ARISTOTLE

CHAPTER I   Criticism of Plato

WHEN Plato died, his work continued in the Academy, the institute of advanced studies he had founded. But it was continued only in part; for while his successors could take over and develop his doctrine, they lacked his inspiration. The most brilliant of his students was perhaps too critical and too original to succeed him; at any rate, Aristotle is known to us as the founder of a second institute in Athens, the Lyceum. His school is more often called the Peripatetic.[1] The first period of his life, spent as a student under Plato, lasted some twenty uneventful years. Subsequently, he was at Assos in Asia Minor as a teacher and at the court of Philip of Macedon as tutor to his son Alexander. During the last phase, he was active in Athens as head of the Lyceum. European thought owes much to the fact that it has two men of such intellectual power at its beginnings, though, interestingly enough, it was in the end not Aristotle who saved us from domination by Plato, but rather Plato who helped to make possible the repudiation of Aristotle's theology. But that is a much later story.

If we were attempting to assess the influence of Aristotle upon posterity, we should be disconcerted at the outset by finding that those works of his that were best known in the ancient world are precisely those that are accessible to us only in fragments, while those with which we are familiar do not appear to have been in circulation on any scale till about the beginning of the Christian era. It is clear evidence of

[1] Because he was supposed to have given his lectures while walking.

Plato's influence on the young scholar that Aristotle's earliest works were in the dialogue form. Werner Jaeger has attempted to trace the development of his thought, taking these dialogues as the starting-point. In them, he is still a Platonist, though his presentation is original and we can see his criticisms beginning to take shape. To this stage belongs also a treatise *Protrepticus,* fragments of which have come down to us; it was written, apparently, in praise of the contemplative life as alone worthy to be called life.

It is typical of the neglect into which these early efforts have fallen that the admirable volume of *Selections* compiled by W. D. Ross leaves them entirely out of account. He concentrates upon the various books that, by their titles, would seem to be meant as systematic treatments of some major theme, such as *Politics* or *Ethics* or *Physics*. Their contents, however, suggest rather that they have been compiled from unpublished or definitely unpolished manuscripts, supplemented by lecture-notes. The table of contents, for example, in the Oxford translation of the *Metaphysics,* shows that Book K is made up of material in part already given in earlier sections of the same book, and partly borrowed from the *Physics*. Again, the nature of substance is considered more than once, and each time as if this were the first occasion. There is something so ragged about these books that we must suppose that they have been pieced together rather than composed. One extreme case is that of the *Ethics,* which has come down to us in two forms, one bearing the name of Aristotle's son Nicomachus and the other that of his colleague Eudemus. The reader who comes to Aristotle expecting to find a clear-cut system that will at once do justice to his own emphasis on logic and account for the authority attached for so long to his name, will be severely disappointed.

If we ask what led Aristotle to break with Plato, one explanation is to be found in the stage reached by the latter's thought when he came into contact with him as a student. Plato was passing from the flowing conversational style of the earlier dialogues to that of the *Timæus,* in which we are rather present at a lecture. With that change in presentation went an enhanced interest in mathematics, in the hope that this would furnish a solution for all problems. It is with this association of the Forms with numbers that Aristotle quarrels particularly; his more general criticisms are no great advance on those that already occurred to Plato himself. Now, it is important to see that Plato does not do with mathematics what the modern physicist does. He does not *apply* mathematics to what he observes, so as to yield a formula that covers a wide range of phenomena; he sets out to *deduce* what can be observed from the properties of numbers and figures. In other words, he seems to have made numbers and figures the actual *stuff* of the world and not merely its structure.

Behind this objection to conferring an absolute value on mathematics lies a difference in the outlook of the two men that has had the most important consequences. Aristotle had an interest in detail that was lacking in Plato; the latter regarded the individual, concrete fact rather as a ladder to be kicked down once one had mounted by it to the universal. Hence we find that sense-perception has a higher value set on it, though, to be sure, Aristotle—to judge from the somewhat inconsistent statements that have come down to us—never quite abandoned the role of the rationalist for that of the empiricist. But here again we must avoid identifying Aristotle's interest in detail with that of the modern scientist. He relied, of course, on observation without experiment, and his observation was keenest because interested in such matters as political constitutions.[2] Statements in physics are often made with no appeal whatsoever to the facts. In biology, to be sure, much of his work is of permanent value. What Aristotle did was to create the various sciences as separate disciplines, leaving it to others to develop them. Yet, as we shall see, he retained to the end the metaphysical interest he had derived from Plato. But perhaps we can never do justice to him, since his dialogues are lost and lecture-notes are a poor substitute for the lecturer himself.

[2] He collected and classified 158 Greek constitutions.

Form and Matter

WE have seen that Plato took over from his predecessors the problem of how to relate the element of change and the element of permanence in our experience. We have also seen that Aristotle was not satisfied with Plato's solution, the theory of Forms. He has two substitutes for this, one dynamic and the other static. An illustration of the former from human life may be helpful. John Smith changes while still remaining John Smith. We use different terms to describe him at the various stages of growth and development, speaking of him as a baby, child, young man, adult, old man and so on. What connects these stages is well expressed in the saying that 'the child is father of the man'. That is to say, he has the capacity to become the man, while the development of what is in the child yields the man. Aristotle would say that the child is potentially the man. So an acorn is potentially what the oak is actually, and the oak is potentially the ship's mast that is made out of it. Modern science makes considerable play with this notion of the potential, what a thing is not as yet but has it in it to become.

The case of the oak that is made into a ship's mast admits of another analysis that is also to be found in Aristotle, that into matter and form. For the felled oak as it lies on the ground is potentially a great many things beside a ship's mast, a dressing-table, a bookcase, and so on. It is, so to say, the material that can be worked up in any one of a number of ways. On the other hand, the mast may have been made out of any one of a number of tree-trunks that were adequate in size and other qualities. It is, we might say, the shape that can be imposed on various different materials. Aristotle would say that the wood is the matter and the mast the form. But he uses this pair of terms in a much wider sense. Thus, if the ship's mast were to be removed on shore and used as a flagstaff, it would become the matter on which the form of a flagstaff was imposed. Equally, 'oak' could be regarded as the form assumed by the matter 'tree', and 'tree' the form assumed by the matter 'plant'. And so we might go on, everything being matter in relation to what is above it in the scale, and form in relation to what is below it.

So we could construct what has been called 'the great chain of being', a conception that powerfully influenced the Western mind till it was displaced last century by another, that of evolution.[3] According to this, everything has its place in a graded series, a hierachy of being, each member of which plays the part of form to what is below it and of matter to what is above it. For the scale to be complete, there must of course be two exceptions to this rule. The highest member will be pure form with nothing above it to which it can serve as matter. Medieval thought was not slow to identify pure form with God, but Aristotle did not make that identification himself. Equally, at the bottom there must be pure matter, with nothing below it to which it can serve as form. That, however, is not to be regarded as a definite existent, but as the point at which our thinking has to call a halt, a limit. It is obvious that this construction has a good deal in common with Plato's vision of the world as a series of stages through which one ascends in love or desire towards Absolute Beauty at the summit.

This brief summary of Aristotle's account of the physical world needs supplementing at one further point, his analysis of the causal concept. He did not, as later thinkers were to do, raise the question what we mean by saying that *a* is the cause of *b* and on what grounds we make such an assertion. He took the causal relation for granted as something with which everyone is familiar, and found that there were four kinds of cause. Let us take as an illustration a house that is in process of building. In the light of what was said above, we can distinguish at once the *material* and the *formal* causes. Under the first head we bring the bricks and mortar, the windows and doors, and everything else that goes into the building. Under the second head we bring the form of a house, represented by the architect's design. For of course the materials we have enumerated might have made something other than a house, a shop or an office, for example. Thirdly, we can

[3] See Arthur O. Lovejoy: *The Great Chain of Being,* 1933.

speak of the *efficient* cause, represented by the contractor and the men under his employ, for without these the materials and the design would not have been brought together, nothing, as we say, would have been 'effected'. Fourthly, there is the *final* cause, the end in view for the whole process. Is the house being built to be occupied, to be sold, or to be let, and if so, to whom? These are questions we ask when we see the work going on.

This is a rough analysis that is valid enough for the purposes of everyday life, though it is too imprecise an instrument for the scientist to employ. Indeed, some physicists seem to make it their aim to dispense with the causal notion altogether. What is of special importance in Aristotle is the emphasis he lays on the *final* cause. "In the history of science, there has been no more strenuous defender of 'final causes'." [4] Now, the Greek thought of nature not as a machine but as an artist, though one that worked unconsciously, no doubt. So Aristotle conceives of nature as a realm of purpose. Each level in the hierarchy of nature fulfils the purpose of the one below it and serves that of the one above it.

> *Striving to be man, the worm*
> *Mounts through all the spires of form.*

This is not evolution as we understand it. For it describes, not a long and bloody process in which species arise and perish, but the erection by nature, out of the inorganic and organic material at her disposal, of a pyramid in which the higher forms rest on those below them.

CHAPTER III   The Soul

WHEN we come to Aristotle's psychology, we shall not expect him to share with Plato the extreme view for which the soul is the immortal tenant of a strange and hostile body. He will think in terms of gradations rather than of sharp distinctions. That is in fact what

[4] D. J. Allan: *The Philosophy of Aristotle,* 1952, p. 46.

we find. He uses here the categories of form and matter, actual and potential, worked out in his study of nature. The soul for him is the form of the body. This does not mean that it is merely the most complex level reached in the development of the material organism, as it might suggest to a modern reader. For, while form and matter are inseparable only in thought and are distinguished *by us* in a substance, form is for Aristotle sovereign over matter. The other set of categories, actual and potential, helps to preserve that relation. The soul is the form of a specific kind of organism, and that organism in turn can most adequately be described as the one that is potentially soul. Aristotle recognizes that, within our experience, the psychological and the physiological are bound together. He knows nothing of the connection between mind and brain, but had he known it he would have said that it entirely supported his view.

His analysis of the soul is akin to that of Plato, which to be sure, was based on certain obvious distinctions. But he is intrigued by one fact that may well not have come within his predecessor's ken. Certain lower forms of life, worms and insects, for example, do not die when they are cut in half; instead, each half continues to function as though it were a whole. The relation between soul and body is not therefore that the former is present spatially in the latter, in which case part of one would carry with it only part of the other. The soul must be present non-spatially, so that it can function as a whole even in the two parts into which the body is divided. Yet, of course, there is a close connection between the soul in certain of its activities and the body in certain of its parts, the sense-organs. We see by the eye, and if the eye is injured, sight is impaired as a result. This might lead us to question the immortality of the soul, were it not that our reasoning powers do not seem dependent on particular organs to the same extent. But that is a question to which we shall come shortly.

What exactly happens in sensation, when, for example, we see a bright or coloured body? One suggestion that had found acceptance in certain quarters was that such a body gave off infinitesimal particles that impinged on the organ of sight. That is too materialistic a view for Aristotle; sensation is rather apprehension of the form of an object and that by a process of appropriation. "Sense is that which is capable of receiving the sensible forms without the matter".[5] Note the qualification 'sensible'; it will be important in the sequel. The illustration used is that of wax taking the imprint of a seal, of whatever metal the seal may be composed. The process of perceiving is one of assimilation, so that not only does the hand become hot from the object it holds—a quite intelligible state of things—but the eye similarly becomes coloured from a coloured object—which is most difficult to grasp. But of course we perceive, let us say, a body that is bright, coloured, heavy, and so on; we pool the findings of the various senses in our awareness of objects. There must therefore be what Aristotle calls 'common sense' to perform this function of collection and synthesis.[6]

We are now in a position to consider the different levels at which the soul functions. For Aristotle, the human soul will not be something quite new; it will represent an advance on the principle of life in animal and plant and at the same time include these. They will be the matter to which it gives its specific form. Thus we must think of the human soul as containing within itself those functions that constitute the soul in animal and plant. Let me again make the point that this does not imply that man has come about by evolution from plant and animal. Each species is fixed and there is no transition from one to another for Aristotle. It is as if a graded series of textbooks on a subject were written at the same time but quite independently; when the series was complete, we should see how each formed an advance on what was in the one below it. So plants possess the nutritive powers of the soul, they seek food to maintain themselves. The animal has these, and in addition is capable of perception; with perception goes desire, and "desire includes appetite, anger, and rational wish".[7] Man in addition has reason.

While reason supervenes upon the lower levels of the soul, it is distinct from them and does not appear to be as closely bound up with the body as they are. What complicates Aristotle's treatment at this point is that he

[5] W. D. Ross: *Aristotle Selections*, 1927, p. 211.
[6] Note how different this use of the term is from our own.
[7] *Ibid.*, p. 205.

distinguishes two types of reason, one active and the other passive, and goes on to relate these as form and matter, actual and potential. As the sense-organ receives the impress of sensible forms, so the passive reason receives that of intelligible forms, e.g., mathematical relations. So far so good. What the active reason does is not so clear. Does it operate on the passive reason and what it receives? That is suggested by the form-matter analogy. Or is it a fresh source of knowledge by intuition and contemplation? That is supported by Aristotle's acceptance of speculation as the highest activity with something divine about it. What is important in this connection is that he claims complete separability from the body and immortality for the active reason alone.

CHAPTER IV   Ethics

WHEN Aristotle turns his attention to moral questions, he does what Plato did and what any Greek would have done; he brings these under the heading of 'the good' rather than 'the right'. That is to say, he is concerned not so much with the obligations men are under as with the ends they seek. What a man seeks is what he regards as 'the good'. The term 'good' is normally relative; a knife is good for cutting, a field for a baseball game, aspirin for relieving headache, etc. Is there, beyond all these things that are good as means, something that is good as an end in itself, good absolutely? If so, it will be the supreme goal of human endeavour. Aristotle thinks there will be general agreement as to what this supreme good is. It is happiness. That, however, does not help much, as there are so many opinions on what constitutes happiness. His own suggestion is that happiness for man lies in the unimpeded exercise of his peculiar function, of what stamps him as a man. In the light of what has been said above, this will be his reason. "If this is the case, human good turns out to be activity of soul in accordance with virtue, and if there are more than one virtue, in accordance with the best and most complete." [8]

[8] *Ibid.*, p. 225.

That the word 'virtue' here has a much wider range than with us is shown by the fact that Aristotle goes on to distinguish between intellectual and moral virtues. Some such translation as 'characteristic excellence' might bring out its meaning better. But before we glance at the intellectual virtues, we shall do well to note how down-to-earth Aristotle's treatment of the good life is. He adds that, in addition to intellectual and moral qualities, it needs also a certain amount of external goods and extension over a whole life. To return now to the intellectual virtues. These are two in number, practical wisdom and theoretical wisdom. The former is our guide in the conduct of life, giving us both general principles and the insight to discern how these are to be applied in particular situations. Aristotle is careful to point out that most men go wrong, not because their principles are mistaken, but because they do not bring particular instances under the general rule they acknowledge. This implies, as he readily allows, that no hard and fast line can be drawn between moral and intellectual virtues. Theoretical wisdom we shall deal with in due course.

We come now to the moral virtues. These are not mere actions, which might be sporadic and not indicative at all of what the person himself is; they are states of character. As such, they are the product of a discipline to which we submit ourselves; but we must have an aptitude for that discipline to begin with. On the dispute between nature and nurture, Aristotle would say that what is present potentially in nature needs to be brought to actuality by nurture.

"Neither by nature, then, nor contrary to nature do the virtues arise in us; rather we are adapted by nature to receive them, and are made perfect by habit." [9]

We form good character by developing good habits, and we form good habits by the repetition of good actions. The process is analogous to that of the flute player who becomes accomplished by constant practice, or, as we should say, the tennis star who never misses a day at the nets. Morality is thus the art of living well, and the good man is the virtuoso.

[9] *Ibid.*, p. 230.

Can we further describe the form this art of living well will take? Yes, we can go on to define virtue as— "a state of character concerned with choice, lying in a mean, i.e., the mean relative to us, this being determined by a rational principle, and by that principle by which the man of practical wisdom would determine it." [10]

Virtue is the mean between two extremes, each of which is bad. Yet the mean is not reached by a mathematical computation, but by tact, a discernment that is itself morally conditioned. The theory appeals at once to the ordinary person, though on examination it turns out to have its difficulties. We can see clearly, for example, that the brave man is one who neither risks his life in foolhardiness nor preserves it at all costs in cowardice. In war, he knows just when he should die at his post and when he should surrender because further struggle is useless. So the miser and the prodigal represent the extremes avoided by the man who knows just when to spend his money and when to save it. But Aristotle admits that there is no word for the man who is neither ambitious, so claiming too much, nor unambitious, not claiming enough. That there is a state of character that keeps the balance we need not doubt.

The important question remains of the highest kind of life and where it ought to be sought. Here Aristotle finds himself pulled in two directions. He lived in a society that called on the citizen to participate in politics, to sit on the jury, and to bear arms in time of war. Yet at the same time it cultivated leisure and the interchange of ideas in conversation. Is action or contemplation the more desirable? Aristotle opts for the latter, while allowing to the former a second and by no means dishonourable place. In the exercise of theoretical reason, in speculation and inquiry, man lives by the highest part of himself, by that which he shares with the gods. It is within man's power to live on earth the immortal life, and let him not refuse to do this, for that would be to surrender to false modesty. But the good citizen who faithfully discharges the duties of his station ranks next in order of merit. The last thing

[10] *Ibid.*, p. 234.

Aristotle wishes to do is to loosen the bonds of society, though he sees—and is he not right in this?—that the highest dimension of life transcends, not the limitations only, but also the duties of society.

CHAPTER V   Politics

ARISTOTLE effects the transition from morals to politics by an argument that does not commend itself to the modern reader, that seems indeed to smack of the totalitarian state. He has said that nature cannot be relied upon to produce virtue, though some contribution from that quarter is indispensable, but that nurture is also necessary. The element of discipline and training is supplied only in part by the family, the most effective portion of it must come from the state and its laws. The state thus takes over for Aristotle the basic moral education of the citizen. It can do that because the state is not in his eyes merely some sort of contractual association into which individuals have entered for the sake of the benefits that will accrue to them therefrom; it is a moral institution and its purpose is the promotion of the good life.

> "If all communities aim at some good, the state or political community, which is the highest of all, and which embraces all the rest, aims at a good in a greater degree than any other, and at the highest good." [11]

Of course, this is not really the totalitarian state; it is, as Aristotle describes it, the larger community that has grown out of the family and tribe and therefore commands a traditional and unforced loyalty.

Though Aristotle does not hesitate, when the moment for it comes, to outline his ideal state, he is much more concerned with analysis and description than with speculation. His common sense attitude revolts against the communist strain in Plato's *Republic*, and he has no sympathy with his abolition of family life and private

[11] *Ibid.*, p. 284.

property in the case of the guardians. More interesting for us is his criticism of one Phaleas of Chalcedon, who maintained that equality of possessions would alone ensure social stability. Once this state of things has been achieved, a uniform system of education should suffice to maintain it. One of Aristotle's criticisms of the theory is as relevant today as then. He points out that wealth is desired, not as an end in itself, but as means to certain ends that are valued for their own sake, such as luxury, pre-eminence, and power. These ends will continue to be sought by other means in a society that has made the use of wealth for this purpose impossible. As he puts it sarcastically: "Men do not become tyrants in order that they may not suffer cold";[12] economic motives are not the only nor always the most powerful ones.

We gather from Aristotle that a question often debated in his day was: What is the best form of government? He himself is not particularly interested in this, because he sees that it is of less importance who possesses power than how it is exercised. Not that these considerations can be entirely divorced; as we shall see, he holds that there is one class in society so placed that it is less likely than others to abuse power. His guiding principle is

> that governments which have a regard to the common interest are constituted in accordance with strict principles of justice, and are therefore true forms; but those which regard only the interest of the rulers are all defective and perverted forms, for they are despotic, whereas a state is a community of free men.[13]

This enables him to divide known forms of government into two main types. The genuine ones are those in which common interest rules, while the spurious ones are ruled by those who seek only their own interest. The examples he quotes of the first are royalty, aristocracy, and constitutional government; of the second dictatorship (as we should say), oligarchy, and democracy. By the last he means a regime in which quality is wholly sacrificed to quantity.

Of these forms of government, the one with which

[12] *Ibid.*, p. 300.
[13] *Ibid.*, p. 302.

Aristotle has most sympathy is that which he calls constitutional. It may be described as a regime in which power lies with the responsible and property-owning members of society. In other words, with the middle class. For Aristotle, a true Greek in this, is anxious to avoid excess: the middle way is best. So he applies his doctrine of the mean to politics as he has already done to ethics. Those who far outstrip their fellows in wealth, personal qualities, or the advantages of birth, are tempted to use these to secure some privileged position for themselves. Those, on the other hand, who are inferior in these respects, are tempted to subversive activities. In either way, the common interest is endangered. It is good therefore that power should rest with the middle class, whose own interest most nearly coincides with the common good. They will bear arms in defense of the state and be competent to make and administer its laws. Even if government rests with a king or a nobility, if the middle class is strong enough it will have to be considered in every act of the rulers and so will give stability to the state.

We saw earlier that Aristotle ascribes to the laws an educative role. "The citizen should be moulded to suit the form of government under which he lives."[14] The state, that is to say, embodies a conception of the good life, moral standards, etc., and it must communicate these to the growing generation. So we realize today that, though we must avoid the indoctrination practiced by the totalitarian states, we are bound to hand on the common convictions by which a democratic society lives. We must educate (we may not like the word 'mould') our children for democracy. The education Aristotle envisages is a liberal one, for in such a state as he has in mind no citizen will need to practice a trade and he will be ashamed to earn money. There are, of course, certain things a man should know for the management of the household or for participation in public business, such as reading and writing. But even the useful arts should be taught, not only because they are useful, but also because they refine and elevate the mind.

[14] *Ibid.*, p. 318.

The highest accomplishments, however, will be those in which a man indulges for their own sake, such as music and philosophy. By these he enters upon a life akin to the divine.[15]

CHAPTER VI   God

WE have seen that what Aristotle did was to break up the total vision of Plato into a number of separate disciplines, each to be worked out in detail and for its own sake. He is, we may say, the father of that specialization that has become at once so fruitful and so dangerous in our time. But the element of vision is by no means lacking from his work. It comes out in what posterity has called his 'metaphysics' (i.e. the work that comes 'after the *Physics*' in the Aristotelian corpus), but what he himself termed 'first philosophy'. Here we find his quest for what Plato sought, that which truly *is*. Unfortunately, his works as they have come down to us do not show any clear solution to this problem: perhaps this was one of the cases in which he drew subtle distinctions that proved too difficult for his students to grasp. We have seen that he analyzed the concrete thing into form and matter. This yields three possibilities. Substance (that which truly is) could be (a), form (b), matter (c) the concrete thing as such. Each of these identifications can be supported from the evidence accessible to us. The one thing that is certain is that he rejected Plato's position, understanding this to mean that what truly is is separate from the actual objects of our experience.

He was, indeed, in a difficulty as soon as he came to ask just what is the object of scientific knowledge. At the beginning of his *Metaphysics* he states one possibility quite clearly. According to this, all our knowledge derives in the last (or shall we say, the first?) resort from sense-impressions, out of which we elaborate general ideas. This would make Aristotle an empiricist. But it is not the only account of knowledge he has

[15] Be it noted that Aristotle's discussion is carried on in complete indifference to Alexander's contemporary creation of a world-empire.

left to us. That was not to be expected in view of the position held by mathematics as an exact science not based on sense-impressions, though relevant to what is known thereby. Aristotle clearly holds that each science rests upon certain general principles that are not to be demonstrated but are apprehended intuitively. Further, he is aware that scientific knowledge is much more than an enumeration of instances, that it is the construction of a generalization that embraces and does justice to all these.

> We suppose ourselves to possess unqualified scientific knowledge of a thing, as opposed to knowing it in the accidental way in which the sophist knows, when we think that we know the cause on which the fact depends, as the cause of that fact and of no other, and, further, that the fact could not be other than it is.[16]

We must allow therefore that something of the rationalist is to be found in Aristotle along with something of the empiricist.

When we come to his cosmology, we find much there that ruled the medieval mind and has entered into Christian theology by that door. Here he was beyond the range of observation and fell back on assumptions that seem to us extraordinarily naïve. Thus, he assumes that there are four elements, of which two, fire and air, 'naturally' move upwards, while the other two, earth and water, as naturally move downwards. He adds to them a fifth element, ether, of which the heavenly bodies are composed, and which will have a 'perfect', i.e., a circular movement. The earth itself is spherical and at the centre of the universe. The heavenly bodies are located on a series of rotating spheres around it, and Aristotle reckons that the total number of spheres will be forty-nine. The whole system is eternal, there was no creation. When Aquinas came to use Aristotle's metaphysics for his natural theology, he had to meet this point. He did so by suggesting that while theoretically, the world *might have been* eternal it was *in fact* created and had a beginning.

It has often been pointed out that while for us motion

<hr>

16 *Ibid.*, p. 25.

is natural and rest has to be explained, for the ancients
the reverse was the case. They saw a cart, so to speak,
and asked where the horse was to move it. The constant and eternal movement of the spheres calls for an
equally eternal source of motion. Only, in this case,
the movement must be original, the First Mover must
himself be exempt from movement and change. Since on
this all else depends, it is the ultimate principle of explanation and so the philospher's equivalent for God.
Be it noted that he is not the Creator, for his eternity
is matched by its. The communication of motion to the
spheres is therefore to be compared, not to a thrust
given to an object from behind, but to the attraction
something desirable exerts upon a mind that contem-
plates it. God moves the world as the object of its
desire. Perhaps, Aristotle says, there was truth in the
ancient myth that the heavenly beings are gods; if so,
we may think of them as aspiring towards God and so
bringing about the movements characteristic of the physical universe. There is surely an element of grandeur in
this picture.

What of God himself, this solitary monarch of the
universe? As he did not create, so he does not exercise
any providential oversight. He is not involved in the
fortunes of the world and the human race, as is the
Christian God; it would seem out of place to pray to
him. He is "a monarch who reigns, but does not rule".[17]
The one hint of divine immanence is in the suggestion
that the highest good is in the world both "as something separate and by itself, and as the order of the
parts".[18] For the Greek, it was axiomatic that the divine
life will be without emotion and will be self-sufficient.
Indeed, among ourselves, a God who *needs* his creation
is known only to the mystics. Inevitably, God is thought
of by Aristotle as enjoying that which for himself was
the highest form of happiness, namely, the activity of
pure thought. But in the case of God there can be
nothing beyond himself to serve as object of his
thought; he must be his own object. His life is therefore described as "a thinking on thinking".[19] Do we say
that this is cold and unattractive? Aristotle would reply

[17] W. E. Greene: *Moira*, 1944, p. 322.
[18] Ross: *Op cit.*, p. 117.
[19] *Ibid*, p. 116.

that that is the case only because we are ourselves absorbed in actions that promise immediate gain and unwilling for the austere adventure of the intellectual life. Were we ready for it, we should find in it a bliss well fitted to symbolize the life of God himself.

For further reading:

Oxford translation; translation of *Metaphysics* in Everyman's Library.

W. D. Ross: *Selections.*
Aristotle.
   D. J. Allan: *Aristotle.*
   A. E. Taylor: *Aristotle.*
   G. R. G. Mure: *Aristotle.*

PART THREE

AUGUSTINE

CHAPTER I   Philosophy and Religion

THE marriage of East and West that was the ambition and achievement of Alexander had its spiritual counterpart in syncretism in religion and eclecticism in philosophy. The various schools and the many gods went into the common pool. Plato contributed much to this welter and Aristotle little—at least the Aristotle known to us. A major contribution was made by Stoicism, whose founder Zeno, though he worked in Athens, was of Phoenician descent. His creed combined a materialist view of the universe with an ethic of self-discipline, restraint of emotion, and indifference to the ills and accidents of life, not excluding death itself. The most important representative of the new and many-sided movement was Posidonius, whose lectures at Rhodes in the second and first centuries B.C. were attended by Pompey and Cicero. His work is largely lost to us, though modern scholarship has done wonders in retrieving it, albeit in fragmentary and tentative condition, from the writings of those whom he influenced, Cicero being our main source. At the beginning of the Christian era, a popular philosophy was current in many forms, and itinerant teachers carried it from city to city.

When Paul at Ephesus hired the lecture-room of one Tyrannus as his centre, he was doubtless regarded by the curious as one more such philosopher, and, if Luke is to be trusted, he was not unwilling to avail himself of this point of contact. The new movement of which he was the missionary had something in common with the philosophy of the time, enough at least to enable it to appeal sometimes to that philosophy as its ally against the follies of pagan religion. But it was more than a philosophy, and it claimed to be more than just another religion bidding for men's allegiance. Rooted as it was in Jewish monotheism, it presented to the world as Lord one who had been rejected by the Jewish leaders and executed by the representative of Roman law. It offered deliverance alike from the demons that mustered in the air and from the passions that lurked within the soul. It appealed to an event—Jesus of Nazareth 'suffered under Pontius Pilate'—and not merely to an idea; it knit those who accepted it into a close fellowship; it called for and made possible a purity of life that seemed even to the Stoic moralist beyond the resources of human nature.

Cradled in Palestine, it grew to manhood in the Greco-Roman world, where many rivals faced it. Few of these were worthy of its steel, and when they offered terms of peace, it refused all talk of compromise and so prevailed. Only in one quarter did it find an opponent of like spiritual calibre. That was Neoplatonism, which produced in the third Christian century the genius of Plotinus as its master-exponent. His vision was of that hierarchy of being to which reference has already been made, with God, the One, the Good at the summit. To him no human words are adequate, him no human mind can grasp; we can only affirm what he is not. Out of the infinite wealth of his being all else proceeds, stage by stage, the world of Forms, the world-soul, man and nature, till we arrive at matter, the point at which being vanishes into nothingness. Man's task is to ascend this scale by virtue, knowledge, and ascetic practices, till in ecstasy he attains to unity with the nameless One. This is 'the flight of the alone to the Alone' of which the mystic speaks with awe.

The Christian Church prevailed over Neoplatonism only by incorporating much of its teaching into its own doctrine, and we shall see that Augustine was responsible for no small measure of this synthesis. For there was a stage in his life at which he needed Neoplatonism to deliver him from Manicheism and so make possible his return to the faith in which his mother Monnica had nurtured him. Mani, the founder of this new religion, taught as a prophet in Persia in the first half of the third Christian century and was put to death by the priests of the official Magian religion. He taught a dualism that identified good with light and evil with darkness. Man is the work of the evil principle at war with the good, and he contains sparks of light imprisoned in matter. Salvation is the deliverance of these sparks, and to achieve this a succession of aeons, Christ being one of them, was sent down from heaven. Hence the inculcation of an ascetic morality, hence also the division of adherents into the elect, who could bear the full weight of these requirements, and the hearers, from whom a lower standard was accepted.

The personality and life of Augustine were played upon by all these spiritual currents in succession. Born in a North African village in A.D. 354 of a Christian mother and a heathen father, he grew up to combine intellectual brilliance with moral laxity. Enslaved by sexual passion, he turned to Manicheism because it relieved him of responsibility; what he was doing was not his own sin but the work of the evil principle within him. After his removal first to Rome and then to Milan, dissatisfied with Manicheism, he toyed for a while with scepticism, but eventually was drawn to the character and preaching of Ambrose, bishop of Milan. His intellectual difficulties were resolved with the help of Neoplatonism. But the crucial difficulty, as he himself saw, was the moral one and there only conversion was of any avail. The reorientation of his life by the Christian faith brought deliverance from the impulses that had tormented and seduced him, and his mother's prayers were answered when he received baptism at the hands of Ambrose. He was to become known to his own day as administrator, teacher, and writer, and to posterity as the greatest and most influential thinker Christianity had produced since New Testament times.

CHAPTER II   Faith and Reason

At his conversion, Augustine was a master of the Latin language and a professor of rhetoric. He had early fallen under the spell of Cicero, and it was the philosophic temperament in him that attracted him to Manicheism, as against what he then considered the crudities of the Bible and Catholic teaching. He had to adjust his new standpoint to what he brought over from his old life; in other words, faith and reason had to come to terms in him. His solution of the problem is expressed once for all in the words: "I believe, that I may understand". If justice is to be done to this, full right must be conceded to faith and understanding alike. Augustine saw that, in the sphere of moral and religious truth, insight is conditioned by the character, that God is to be seen by the pure in heart alone. He is to be known by those who love him, not by those who examine him curiously. As he had learned, the riches of the Christian faith are accessible only to those who are within the Christian communion. So much for faith. But he who believes must go on to bring to bear upon his faith all the intellectual powers that God has given him, that he may arrive at a Christian philosophy that will satisfy the mind as well as the heart.

For one brief period, it is true, Augustine had toyed with scepticism. Perhaps the quest of truth was vain, and led nowhere in the end. But his acute mind soon grasped the fallacy inherent in this position. It is in fact self-destructive, for does not the truth that there is no truth fall under condemnation? But he saw that something more than a logical fallacy was involved, that scepticism was an assault upon life itself and upon the certainty it so sorely needs. The strength of scepticism lies in its power to challenge every particular assertion we make: is there one so fundamental as to resist its attack? Yes, there is, and Augustine anticipated Descartes in his discovery of the certainty that is inherent in self-consciousness. That is to say, however much I may doubt, I cannot doubt that I doubt, and therefore that I am. This ultimate certainty is much more than a successful argument, for he who discovers it is himself involved. He builds his life anew on the conviction that doubt is only possible in a world that contains truth, and that, the more agonizing the doubt, the more precious the truth once it is found.

This enables us to understand Augustine's argument for God's existence, as set out in his treatise *On Free Will*. It is not in fact an argument in the strict sense of the term, but it is none the worse for that. It is an analysis of human experience. Man shares with the animals in existence, life, and intelligence, but in virtue of his reason he transcends them. Whereas sense-knowledge enables the possessor to deal with the particular features of the world that impinge upon him at a given time, reason makes it possible for him to grasp its universal and permanent features. It is true that at the level of reason men differ, as witness the schools of philosophy. Yet common to all is the conviction that truth is and that it is desirable. Nay more, there are some principles that are self-evident and secure universal acknowledgment: we do not argue with the man who denies them, we question his sanity. There is therefore a realm of spiritual values that we recognize as independent of ourselves and as claiming our homage. This does not require God to support it from outside: "truth itself is God".[1] In other words, he is not one truth among others, not even the highest of all; he is "that sole Truth by which all things are true".[2]

Now the God to whom Augustine worshipped was the Triune god of the Christian faith. He accepted him as such because he had made himself known as such by revelation. But here if anywhere was a challenge to one who was resolved to go on from faith to understanding. How was the doctrine of the Trinity to be made intelligible? The Greek Fathers had had recourse for this purpose to analogies drawn from nature, e.g., the sunlight that is one in the sun, the ray, and the apex of the ray. Everyone is familiar with St. Patrick's use of the shamrock. It was the great merit of Augustine that he went for his analogies to psychology and personal relations. Thus, he bids men turn their minds in upon themselves, when they will see that man is a unity of three things, existence, knowledge, and will. Or he can analyze the mind into memory, understanding, and will. But the most effective of his analogies is that in which he identifies the Father with love, the Son with the object of love, and the Spirit with the bond of love uniting the two. Yet he is ready to acknowledge that all such illustrations drawn from human life are mere stop-gaps; we speak of God thus, not that we may assert anything, but that we may not remain silent.

The Christian doctrine of creation, too, called for con-

[1] Augustine: *Earlier Writings,* trans. H. S. Burleigh, 1953, p. 159.
[2] *Confessions,* trans. F. J. Sheed, 1945, p. 187.

sideration by one who thought naturally in Neoplatonic terms. We have seen that Augustine does not regard God as an external support to the realm of eternal spiritual values. Equally, he does not regard him as such in his relation to the realm of forms or patterns in accordance with which, in Plato's *Timæus,* the world was made. In each case, the universals are more than objects for the mind of God, they are aspects of his being. Before God's face "stand the causes of all things transient with the changeless principles of all things that change, and the eternal reasons of all the things of unreason and of time".[3] God's self-knowledge is at the same time the knowledge of the structure of his creation, and that includes within it the knowledge of why the detail of creation is what it is. Creation came about, he says, elsewhere, by the production of all things in germ, whereupon their development followed as God ordained. God made the 'seminal causes', which "are germs of things or invisible powers or potentialities, created by God in the beginning in the humid element and developing into the objects of various species by their temporal unfolding".[4] The theory results from the application of Neoplatonism to the text of Gen i.

Augustine's conception of faith and understanding clearly presupposes that the human mind is not thrown entirely on its own resources in its quest for truth, but that it operates in a world prepared by God for an encounter between him and men. As the name of 'exemplarism' had been given to the previous doctrine, according to which the principles and patterns of things pre-exist eternally in God, so we are accustomed to call 'illuminism' the suggestion that the mind and what it knows are alike bathed in a supernatural light and that only so is knowledge possible. One is reminded at once of such a verse as "In thy light shall we see light",[5] and also of the passage in the *Republic* in which the Good is likened to the sun as the source at once of why things are and of how we are able to know them. For Augustine, just as the eye sees objects in the world through the medium of light, so the mind

3 *Ibid.*, p. 5.
4 Frederick Copleston: *A History of Philosophy* 1950, II, 76.
5 Psalm xxxvi. 9.

is able to apprehend the eternal verities through the medium of an illumination divinely given. Perhaps we may say that for him spiritual truth is not something man discovers, nor is it merely revealed; it is apprehended in the interplay of man's seeking and God's self-disclosure.

CHAPTER III   Against the Manichees

THE attraction of Manicheism for Augustine lay in the fact that it offered a solution of the age-long problem of evil. And who would not welcome that? The Christian teaching of the Catholic Church (the great Church as opposed to the numerous heretical or schismatic groups) asserted that the world had been made by one good God: how then did it come to contain so much imperfection? To be sure, an explanation was provided, in the form of an incredible story in which a serpent played a prominent part and the fruit of a forbidden tree was eaten. But this tale was only one of many in the Old Testament, a book whose conception of God was crude and whose morality was more than doubtful. Manicheism seemed to Augustine more rational because it appealed to principles and was not committed to any stories about the past: even the story of Jesus was for it a veil that obscured the truth. He could only reconcile himself to the Old Testament when he became familiar with the allegorical method of interpretation current in the Church; also when he understood that revelation takes cognizance of the historical situation of the recipient, is progressive, as we should say.

What the Manichean solution of the problem of evil was has been indicated already. It employed the concept of substance, and that in a materialist sense, and it borrowed from the Persian religion of the time the opposition between two principles, one good and the other evil. The materialist bias in the system made it present the two under the image of two substances that touch at one side, while on the other side the good substance extends indefinitely. Every human being is of mixed composition and the evil he does is ultimately the work of a bad principle within him. On this theory,

God remains unquestionably good, and evil originates elsewhere than in him; but since that elsewhere is matter, it follows that there is no deliverance from it this side of death, except the relative deliverance possible to the few who can abstain from meat and wine, and can eschew sexual intercourse and the procreation of children—for does not this increase the number of light-sparks imprisoned in matter?

It was scarcely possible that a person of Augustine's inquiring disposition and intellectual powers should remain content with such a system. Disillusionment came when a spokesman for it, one Faustus, proved specious and unconvincing. One argument in particular always seemed to Augustine to dispose of the Manichean dualism. It was axiomatic with Mani, as with almost everyone else in the ancient world, that God is not subject to change; as it was put, he is incorruptible. In that case, how could he be in such danger from the evil principle as to be drawn into conflict with it in order to preserve the kingdom of light against the assaults of darkness? In modern language, a dualism in which one member is God and so infinite is inconceivable. There are only two possibilities. *Either* the good principle is infinite, in which case the evil principle is finite (there cannot be two infinites), and then there is no dualism. *Or* the good principle is finite, in which case there is dualism, but it (the good principle) is not at all what we mean by 'God'. But, of course, it was not sufficient to show that this solution was unsatisfactory; the problem of evil remained, and another solution had to be found.

Augustine sought and found it in two directions at the same time, from Neoplatonism and from Catholic Christianity. The first rendered him the great service of freeing him from the materialist thinking of the Manichees. He describes his own condition at this stage:

> I was so gross of mind—not seeing even myself clearly—that whatever was not extended in space, either diffused or massed together or swollen out or having some such qualities or at least capable of having them, I thought must be nothing whatsoever.[6]

Neoplatonism made possible for him a purely spiritual

conception of God and also of evil. The latter was not another thing alongside of God, opposing him and limiting him. It was the absence of being, the privation of good, and as such dependent on the prior existence of good. It is negative and not positive. But how does this defect come about in a universe that is *ex hypothesi* (for the Neoplatonist) perfect? The answer is that a defect in the part ministers to the perfection of the whole. "The fact that there are souls which ought to be miserable because they willed to be sinful contributes to the perfection of the universe".[7]

Because they willed to be sinful—has not Augustine changed his ground entirely at this point? He has. He has exchanged the Neoplatonic for the Biblical point of view. Man possesses free will by God's gift that he may use it for God and in obedience to him; sin arises when he turns God's gift against the giver, chooses the lower rather than the higher, sets up as lord of his own life. This is the momentous insight of Augustine, that should have led him beyond all talk of evil as mere negation and privation. A bayonet charge and a concentration camp are not to be explained as mere absence of good. Man sins, not because he in entangled in matter, but because in the mysterious exercise of his freedom he so wills. And the conflict within him is not between two substances or two principles, but between two wills; and those two wills are but the forms one will assumes that it may evade the good it sees but dreads. That was Augustine's own reading of his experience:

When I was deliberating about serving the Lord my God, as I had long meant to do, it was I who willed to do it, I who was unwilling. It was I. I did not wholly will, I was not wholly unwilling. Therefore I strove with myself and was distracted by myself.[8]

[6] *Confessions*, p. 102.
[7] *Earlier Writings*, p. 186.
[8] *Confessions*, p. 137.

CHAPTER IV   Against the Donatists

WE of the present day find it difficult to think ourselves into an atmosphere in which the Manichean dualism could flourish and even win the allegiance of an Augustine. The case is different with the Donatist controversy, for here we are reminded at once of the bitterness attendant upon occupation and liberation in several European countries only a few years ago. In the final efforts of the Roman state to stamp out Christianity in North Africa, there were those who yielded to the demand to surrender copies of Scripture and hence were termed *traditores* by those who refused. When the persecution was over and these returned to the Church, were they to be readmitted or not? And what was to be done with those who had handed over other books pretending they were the Scriptures? Or who had a certificate from a complaisant official to the effect that they had handed them over when they in fact had done nothing of the kind? The Donatists insisted that the true Christians must have nothing to do with anyone who was under suspicion of having played traitor in time of stress, particularly if he were bishop or priest. Indeed, one who had been baptized by such a person would need to be rebaptized were he admitted to the Donatist Church, though himself quite innocent of apostasy. Thus, in the beginning of the fourth century, a Donatist Church with its hierarchy and sacraments faced the Catholic Church in North Africa and claimed to be the one true Church of Christ.

The dispute, of course, was not purely theological. It was in part an African protest against a Church too closely bound up with imperial Rome. It was also a social protest on the part of the less fortunate elements of society against the officials, the landowners, and the clergy who joined forces with them as members of the privileged class benefiting by Roman rule. On both grounds, some of the wilder elements of the population flocked to the Donatist banner and there were grave disturbances of public peace.

Augustine met his opponents with theological arguments, though we shall see that in the end he pleaded for more forcible means of persuasion. There were in reality two points at issue between him and them.

The first was that of the *unity* of the Church. The Donatist Church was a local body that had cut itself off from the world-wide Christian communion: as such it stood condemned in Augustine's eyes. For him it was axiomatic that the ecumenical fellowship, as we would call it today, is in the right as against the merely provincial one. The whole, he urges, is superior to its parts. He went so far as to declare that there could be no charity where the unity of the Church was not kept. Augustine was not one of those thinkers for whom truth is to be followed against the world. To be quite fair to him, let us say that whatever his theory on this point, in time of trial he would doubtless have stood the test.

The other question was that of the *purity* of the Church. There will always be a tension between the effort to preserve the purity of the Christian Church by confining its membership to those who reach and maintain a certain standard, and the desire to make the conditions of membership such as will bring as many as possible within its influence. A free church tends in the first direction, an established church in the second—I say only 'tends', of course. Augustine, as we shall say, recognizes that wheat and tares are mingled together in the Church's field, but cannot follow the Donatists in their attempt to decide under which head each growth, each member, that is, comes. He would find the holiness of the Church rather in its quality as a whole (i.e. as the sphere in which grace is at work, especially through the sacraments) than in the virtue of its individual members.

He sincerely endeavoured to win the Donatists by persuasion. In so doing, he worked out a view of the sacraments that was based on a distinction between their validity and the benefit they confer. A sacrament, whether of baptism or of ordination, was valid even in the schismatic body like the Donatists, and therefore did not need to be repeated on their return to the Catholic Church. But its benefit was, as it were, held in suspense till they returned to its communion, only becoming effective then. In the end, however, he lost patience and appealed to the State to put down his opponents by force. His sophistical use of the text "Compel them to come in" is notorious. No doubt, he was unconscionably provoked, since the Donatists themselves had recourse to force. No doubt, too, there were cases in which men were kept within the Donatist fold by pressure and welcomed the counter-pressure that released them. If we judge Augustine by the standards of his time, we may well decide to exonerate him. But he is too great a man for such a judgment to suffice. Those who make history must accept responsibility before it.

CHAPTER V   Against the Pelagians

PERHAPS the Pelagian controversy was the most important of those in which Augustine was engaged, though it was the one in which his victory was least decisive. The antagonists differed profoundly in their personal experience and therefore as profoundly in their understanding of man and his relation to God. Pelagius was a monk (perhaps, but not certainly, from an Irish monastery) to whom the control of impulse by the moral judgment presented no difficulty and whose strong moral sense revolted against the license of a time in which a semi-heathen population was only slowly accustoming itself to Christian standards. He therefore stressed responsibility, teaching that it is in man's power to fulfil the Law, since otherwise God would have mocked us in giving it to us and requiring obedience from us. Augustine, on the other hand, had struggled in vain for years against a powerful sex-impulse, only winning deliverance from it when he surrendered to the grace of God in Christ. The change then wrought in him was so drastic that he could ascribe no credit for it to himself; when he was not willing to be chaste, the grace of God had empowered his will to do what otherwise was beyond his power.

In the conflict with Pelagius, Augustine gave definitive form to the doctrines of original sin and predestination. In the formulation of the first of these, he was misled by an error in the Latin version of Rom. v. 12 that he worked with. For "so death passed unto all men, for that all sinned", it had "so death passed unto all men, in whom (Adam) all sinned". He therefore thought of Adam as an inclusive personality, in whose sin all his descendants to the end of time participated, so that even the infant who dies at birth has yet a share in the guilt of the first sin. Further, the sin committed in Eden vitiated the whole nature of man, so that each individual is born predisposed to sin and enslaved in will as well as burdened with guilt. From this condition only a divine intervention can save, and such an intervention must be irresistible, as man cannot contribute anything from his side. Since, as a matter of observation, all do not receive the grace that saves, God must choose to whom to give it and from whom to withhold it, and, since all are equally undeserving, the ground of discrimination must be sought solely in his sovereign will. He elects whom he will to eternal life and abandons whom he will to eternal death. *That* God is righteous, even under these conditions, we must believe; *how* he is righteous, we cannot hope to understand.

The interest of Pelagius, we may say, was moral; he was concerned to emphasize freedom and responsibility as preconditions of right conduct. The interest of Augustine, on the other hand, was religious; he wanted to preserve intact the rights and claims of grace. The issue at stake was apparently settled when Pelagius was condemned as a heretic, first at Carthage in 418 and then at Ephesus in 431. But it was only apparently settled, for the position at which the Church finally arrived can be described either as Semi-Pelagian or as Semi-Augustinian, according to which element in the compromise one emphasizes. Salvation is neither by grace alone nor of man's freedom alone, but by the co-operation of the two. That seems a sensible enough solution, but it has never satisfied those who are really in earnest either morally or religiously. As we shall see, the controversy appeared again at the Reformation, with Erasmus and Luther as the antagonists. In the seventeenth century Jansen rediscovered Augustine, while the Jesuits championed a Semi-Pelagianism in which grace was allotted a much less conspicuous share.

The crux of the controversy has always been the emphasis of one party on freedom in the interests of morality and its limitation by the other in the interests of grace. The Pelagians were able to cite against Augustine some of the passages in his anti-Manichean works, where he had been concerned to show that sin originates with the will and is not any kind of substance or thing. In his debate with them, he tries to save the situation by distinguishing between the will as freedom to choose (which he grants) and as power to act on what one has chosen (which he denies). The latter must be supplied by God's grace. "The good that I would, I do not; the evil that I would not, that I do." It is a common and agonizing experience. But why do we not possess the power to do what we will? In his account of his own conversion, Augustine tells us why, and he is to be followed there rather than in his argument against Pelagius. He had "only to will to go—but to will powerfully and wholly". "For in that matter, the power was the same thing as the will, and the willing *was* the doing."

In other words, the situation in which we cannot do what we will, is not, in the last resort, a misfortune that has come upon us. It *is* because we will it. To be divided is preferable to being committed, because it gives us both the evil we do and the good we approve. So long as he was in this state, Augustine had the pleasures of indulgence combined with the approval of chastity. He was transformed when he gave up this attempt to have the best of both worlds and identified himself unreservedly with one. He willed "powerfully and wholly". Yet he only so willed because he responded to the grace of God he had hitherto refused. For God's grace does not add something to our freedom it does not originally possess; it acts by enabling us to be truly and fully free. There, it would seem, lies the solution of the problem Pelagius raised.

If that is so, then (and here we must revert to Augustine's own view) there is a still higher stage of freedom open to us by God's grace. It is that at which we so yield ourselves to him in love and devotion that we no longer sin. It is our meat and drink to do his will. We *cannot* sin, not in the sense that some power prevents our doing so even if we want, but in the sense that we do not want. Of this supreme freedom Christ is the pattern, and to this the blessed in heaven will surely attain.

CHAPTER VI

The City of God

We have seen Augustine as a controversialist, at grips with the Manichees outside the Church and the Donatists and Pelagius within. So many-sided and historically fruitful is this man's genius, that there is much more that demands our attention. Space requires us to select for consideration one point only, and that must be his interpretation of history. His great work *The City of God* grew up over fifteen years and the final achievement may well have been different from what was originally planned. The occasion for its composition was the sack of Rome by Alaric in 410, an event as catastrophic to the world of that day as the destruction of London by nuclear weapons will perhaps one day be to the British Commonwealth. There were those who contrasted the glories of Rome under paganism with its humiliation as a Christian city and argued that the new religion was responsible for its fall. In replying to them, Augustine launched out upon an exposure of the worst features in the old Roman religion, inferring that it could not possibly have been responsible for the city's rise to imperial greatness. He pointed out, too, that the churches were respected by the conquerors and that, in any case, the Christian does not set his hope on this world or this life.

The permanent message of the book is, of course, not in these contentions but in its brilliant analysis of history as the conflict of two cities, embodying incompatible types of love.

Two loves therefore, have given original (*sic*) to these two cities; self-love in contempt of God unto the earthly, love of God in contempt of oneself to the heavenly; the first seeks the glory of men, and the latter desires God only as the testimony of the conscience, the greatest glory. That glories in itself, and this in God. . . . That boasts of the ambitious conquerors, led by the lust of sovereignty: in this every one serves other in charity, both the rulers in counselling and the subjects in obeying.[9]

The conflict between these two cities begins with Cain and Abel and runs through all history since. We must be careful how we identify the two cities with empirical institutions, for the contrast is rather between two impulses in every man, two tendencies in every institution. Sometimes, to be sure, this world is pitted against the next, sometimes the Roman Empire against the Christian Church; but the conception itself is too grand for any such identification to be finally satisfactory. Augustine sees history, let us say, as a sphere of moral decision because in it there is being worked out a purpose of God men are free to accept or reject.

The idea of love plays so important a part with Augustine that it is necessary at this point to turn aside to consider it briefly. Love as he understands it is compounded of Neoplatonic and Biblical elements. *Caritas* (to use his word, from which the 'charity' of the A.V. at 1 Cor. xiii is derived) includes on the one hand man's aspiration towards God as the supreme good, the satisfaction of the desire for happiness innate in man; on the other hand, it comes about by a humble response to the love with which God in Christ has sought men out and given himself for them. He distinguishes between love as enjoyment and as use, that is, between loving something as an end in itself and loving it as a means to something else for the sake of which it is valued. Only the former kind of love is appropriate where God is the object. Created objects, on the other hand, can only be used aright as they are used for God's sake, and God is to be found by turning from them. It is accordingly our love of God that he has in mind when he bids us "love and do what we please".

If in the eternal order the supreme good is God himself, in the temporal order it is his blessing of peace. While in its fulness peace is something possible only in heaven, some measure of it is within our reach here below. "The good of peace is generally the greatest wish of the world, and the most welcome when it comes."[10] Peace is much more than the absence of

[9] *The City of God,* trans. Healey (Temple Classics edition), III, p. 36f.
[10] *Ibid.,* III, p. 139.

strife; it is the right ordering of the social whole in all its parts, and as such is the work of justice. So that a wholly unfavourable judgment on Rome is not permissible; if the imperial city sinned by pride and cruel ambition, it gave law and peace to the civilized world. The State, we may say, is the product at once of what is worst in man, his insatiable will to power, and of what is best in him, his untiring quest for justice. Alongside of the absolute good that is the aim of religion, Augustine therefore recognizes a relative good that is the work of the secular community.

That *The City of God* was appealed to to furnish a sanction for the medieval papacy cannot be doubted; what we may well doubt is whether this use of its argument is justified. For, let it be said again, the two cities that divide between them the allegiance of mankind are not to be identified with any observable institutions. The City of God is not the Roman Church with its claim to represent God on earth. The latter is a mixed society, the true souls within which are known only to God.

> Let this city of God's remember, that even amongst her enemies, there are some concealed, that shall one day be her citizens: nor let her think it a fruitless labour to bear their hate until she hear their confession, as she hath also (as long as she is in this pilgrimage of this world) some that are partakers of the same sacraments with her, that shall not be partakers of the saints' glories with her, who are partly known, and partly unknown.[11]

Here we have the distinction between the Church visible and the Church invisible that was to fortify Protestantism in its revolt against the medieval hierarchy. For the genius of Augustine was so rich and many-sided that each of the two great divisions within the Western Church can appeal with justice to his authority.

[11] *Ibid.*, I, p. 42.
For further reading:
Translations in the *Library of Christian Classics*.
R. W. Battenhouse (ed.): *A Companion to the Study of St. Augustine*.

PART FOUR
AQUINAS

CHAPTER I   Faith and Reason

In the opening chapter of his *History of Europe,* H. A. L. Fisher finds the basis of European unity in its acceptance, however superficial, of the Christian faith. That is to say, Europe is Christendom from the perspective of the historian. The Turks, domiciled geographically in Europe for centuries, were never admitted to its community of peoples, while the Magyars and the Finns, racially so different from Latin and Teuton, were at home within it once they became Christian. Among the architects of this Christian civilization as it took shape in the Middle Ages, Augustine must be given a high place. His *City of God,* we are told, was favourite reading for Charlemagne, whose empire was as at once the heir of an ancient civilization and nominally, at least, dedicated to God by its obedience to the Christian Church. The new European nations were initiated into the language, the law, and the culture of Rome as they were baptized into the Christian Church. The medieval society that thus arose reached its consummation in art in the Gothic cathedral, in literature in the *Divine Comedy,* and in theology in the *Summa* of Aquinas.

At the moment when this Christian civilization began to take shape in the West, a power rose in the East that was one day to bring it near to destruction. This was the power of Islam. The conquest of the Persian Empire by the Arabs gave them access to a culture, that of the Greeks, of which the West preserved only some fragments. The Abbasid Caliphs made Bagdad the centre of a brilliant civilization in which literature was patronized and science flourished while Europe was passing through the Dark Ages. As Islam marched victoriously along the coast of North Africa, to establish itself in Spain, it brought to Christendom not only an armed threat and a spiritual challenge, but also the possibility of intellectual renewal. What we are here concerned with is the new knowledge of Aristotle, sometimes in translations into Latin from a previous Arabic translation, and sometimes directly in the Greek. The schools in which Christian theology was taught could no more refuse to reckon with Aristotle than their successors in the nineteenth century could evade the challenge of Darwin's work. The *Physics* and *Ethics* might have been accepted without difficulty; the trouble lay with the *Metaphysics*, with its remote God, the world eternal, and the soul probably not immortal in any Christian sense.

Nor was that all. With Aristotle came his Arabian commentators, whose interpretation was usually of a wholly unacceptable order. The first reaction to the new knowledge was therefore understandably hostile, and in 1215 it came under the ban of the University of Paris. In 1231 the opposition was strengthened by a papal prohibition. By this time Thomas Aquinas was teaching in Paris and set himself, while opposing any interpretation of Aristotle that was contrary to the faith, to demonstrate the possibility of one quite compatible with that faith. The victory he secured was of far-reaching consequence. It was in effect the reconciliation of science and religion as they were then known, and the synthesis thus achieved commands the allegiance of some of the ablest minds to this day. Thomism, as it is called, has been declared the official philosophy of the Roman Church, and it has shown an amazing power of adaptation to the needs of the modern world. What Aquinas created was a two-story system that at once gave expression to, and consolidated intellectually, a civilization whose substructure was Roman and whose superstructure was Catholic Christian.

It is open to question whether his triumph was wholly beneficial. Dante associates with him in Paradise his contemporary Bonaventura, and some of us may wish that he rather than Thomas had been followed. For Bonaventura was a Franciscan and Thomas a Dominican, and there was not a little in the former of Francis's love of nature as a system of signs whereby God reveals

62

himself. His inspiration was Platonic and Augustinian, and he did not attempt the sharp separation of theology and philosophy that Thomas effected. For him the truth was a whole and to be apprehended by the whole person. Aquinas, on the other hand, might be accused of introducing into Christian thought in the West a specialization from which it has suffered acutely ever since. Yet he is not to be blamed entirely for this, as he owed much to his forerunner, the Jewish scholar Maimonides, who had laid Aristotle under contribution for the defense and exposition of Judaism. What Maimonides and Aquinas did was to recognize philosophy as a separate discipline governed by reason as theology is by faith and authority. In many cases, no doubt, the philosopher and the theologian will be the same person (at least in the condition with which Aquinas was familiar), but he will as it were hold his faith in suspense while he thinks and writes *qua* philosopher.

This is the problem of reason and faith that we met with in Augustine, but it receives now a solution in accordance with that two-levels pattern that governs the thinking of Aquinas. Philosophy deals, among other topics, with some of those questions that are also the concern of theology, but it employs its own method, that of free rational inquiry and argument. We tend to regard it as a restriction upon philosophy thus understood (or, as we should say, metaphysics) that it recognizes theology as its queen and serves it. But this did not appear to Aquinas as a restriction, because he was so sure that reason and faith could not finally conflict. God is one and therefore truth is one. If what is deduced by the metaphysician from first principles clashes with what the theologian finds in the Bible, it is for both to retrace their steps till they see which has erred and where. Perhaps the philosopher has drawn an invalid inference from an undoubted truth, perhaps the theologian has misunderstood his authority. Aquinas reflects the confidence of a Christian civilization that knew itself to be in possession of the truth.

I HAVE spoken of Aquinas's thought as functioning at two levels, one that of classical antiquity and the other that of the Christian Church. This comes out with particular clarity in the distinction he established between natural theology, which is within the province of philosophy, and a theology of revelation, to be received by faith. To put it simply, but perhaps not crudely, truths about God fall under two heads. There are those, such as the Incarnation and the Trinity, that would be unknown to us had they not been revealed: there are others, such as God's existence and the soul's immortality, that we can reach by our own reasoning powers. Recent developments in Protestant theology, especially on the Continent, tend to deny the possibility of any knowledge of God by reason. But Aquinas would reply that Plato and Aristotle are evidence enough that such knowledge has in fact been reached. There seems to be only one way in which the distinction can legitimately be invalidated, and that is by denying that there is such a thing as unaided human reason; man seeks God always amid God's self-revelation.

The most important of the truths of natural theology is that of God's existence. Western thought has spent a good deal of its energy on the quest for a demonstration that God *is*. As we shall see, it was reserved for Kant to argue that in this his predecessors had been following a will o' the wisp. In some respects, the most fascinating of all the arguments is the one that Aquinas repudiated, and that stands to the credit of an Archbishop of Canterbury, Anselm, though he was not an Englishmen but an Italian. It is known as the ontological argument, for it asserts that the very presence of the idea of God in men's minds is ground enough for claiming that he is. It is the translation of worship into logic. In the moment of adoration, God is the indubitable reality, so that it is impossible to consider even for a moment that he might not be. So long as Aquinas knelt before the altar, he was in agreement with Anselm; but when he rose from his knees and examined the philosophical concept of God he did not find it charged with the same certainty. In this he was surely right.

Anselm was a Platonist, for whom pure thought is the guide to what is; Aquinas an Aristotelian, who set out from sense-perception. God, he held, must and can be demonstrated from the main features of the world as sense-experience reveals these to us. Hence his famous 'Five Ways' to God. The first is borrowed from Aristotle, and urges that no motion, no change, is self-explanatory; there must be an ultimate source of change that is itself unchanging. The second sets out from the fact that we are accustomed to ask of every event what its cause is, and can if we so wish treat the cause as in turn calling for explanation in terms of some previous cause of which it is the effect. Are we to carry the process back indefinitely? Surely not. Rather must we assume the existence of a First Cause. Thirdly, we live in a world of brute fact each item in which might well have been otherwise, might indeed not have been at all. It was under no necessity to be so or even to be. This state of things is only rendered tolerable to the mind if we assume a Being that of necessity is, and so can give ground and substance to everything else. In the fourth place, since the world is a graded series (we have met this concept of the 'great chain of being' more than once before), we must suppose at its apex a perfection that is the source of all else. Finally, there is evidence of design in nature, and this must be due, not to nature itself, but to a designing mind.

What value Aquinas himself attached to these arguments is a historical question with which we need not here concern ourselves. What value do they possess for us? How far can we consider the proofs cogent? It is not possible to take them as settling the question once for all, as there is as much genuine doubt since Aquinas as there was before him. That a strict demonstration of God is not possible, Kant will show. Probably it is not even desirable. Are we then to take the 'five ways' as indicating varying degrees of probability? Or as explicating and supporting a faith already reached on quite different grounds? Or as symbolizing, under the form of demonstration, a reality that lies beyond all demonstration? These are readings of the arguments that would reject them as proofs, while still allowing to them considerable force. They give rational expression to what lies deeper than mere reasoning, e.g., the quest for the permanent amid change, for the ultimate source of our uncertain being, and for the perfection that enters into, yet transcends, all earthly satisfactions.

In any event, the theology of Aquinas represents an amazing *tour de force*, since he tries to identify the God of Aristotle with the God of the Bible. Natural theology leads us to the God whom Christians worship. Perhaps, if pressed, Aquinas would have said that he meant no more than some of his recent expositors have said he meant, that philosophy gives us an empty form that Christian faith subsequently fills up with content. Nineteenth century Protestant theology in the person of Albrecht Ritschl was to regard this fusion of faith and metaphysics as the betrayal of the Gospel. In comparison with the Heavenly Father of whom Jesus spoke, the self-centred God of Aristotle is, he averred, a mere idol, and a most unattractive one at that. If that is so, then the whole labour of medieval theology stands condemned. A more generous view becomes possible once we allow, as I would, that the great mystery of the Godhead is not to be reached by one way only. He transcends both the philosopher's reflection and the effort of faith to find a language in which to express itself. We approach him by both paths and he is at the point where they converge. We never reach that point but our journey is always towards it.

CHAPTER III   Our Knowledge of God

ARISTOTELIAN as Aquinas was, the influence of Neoplatonism on his thinking is unmistakable and pervasive. That influence was mediated to him in part by Augustine and in part more directly by a writer who can claim to have perpetrated one of the most successful literary forgeries. He was the fifth-century monk who wrote under the name of Dionysius the Areopagite, Paul's convert at Athens, and whose work came therefore to be accepted as virtually of apostolic authority. Medieval scholars before Aquinas had translated some of Dionysius's writings from Greek into Latin and commented on them, and he himself produced a commentary on one of them, the *Divine Names*. A modern Catholic scholar's judgment upon Dionysius is of interest: "Personally I consider that the writings are orthodox in regard to the rejection of monism: but that on the question of the Blessed Trinity it is highly questionable at least if they can be reconciled with orthodox Christian dogma".[1] We are not here concerned with Dionysius's orthodoxy, however, but with his contribution to the vexed question of how and in what language we may speak of God. God is he in speaking of whom all language breaks down. Yet we must speak of him. How then shall we do this?

There are, suggested Dionysius, two ways in which we may speak of God and not altogether miss the truth. One is the positive way, by which we ascribe to God all the perfections that experience brings within our reach. So we speak of him as great and wise, good and loving. The other is the negative way, by which we deny to him all that is imperfect. This second method carries us very far indeed, for imperfection attaches not only to our obvious shortcomings, such as rage and malice, but even to our highest virtues and achievements. God transcends our justice and our compassion to such an extent that it might be better to deny them to him than to predicate them of him. Not, to be sure, that we thereby declare him unjust or cruel, but that we bow in awe before a reality that outsoars our highest flight. God is, as we say nowadays, the Wholly Other. It is clear that this position is a dangerous one, and the danger is increased when one prefers, as Dionysius did, the negative way to the positive as less inadequate to God. It is the merit of Aquinas that he guarded against this danger by his doctrine of analogy, while at the same time offering a better criterion of our statements about God.

The principle of analogy avoids two extremes, the first being that terms have the same meaning (are univocal) when used of God as when used of things, and the second that they have nothing in common in the two uses (are equivocal). To assert that God is great or good or wise in the same sense in which a human being is would be disastrously misleading, to

[1] F. Copleston: *History of Philosophy*, 1950, II, p. 92.

say the least. But would it not be equally misleading to use such terms of him on the understanding that they then have nothing in common with goodness and wisdom as we know them? We may therefore ascribe to God that which is highest in our experience in the assurance that there is that in God which does really correspond to this, though separated from it by the distance by which the divine transcends the human. We can thus pass from ourselves to God, daring to predicate of him what is in us, because we derive from him in the first instance, and therefore what is in us is a pale copy and shadow of what it originally and for ever in him.

The principle of analogy can be established by no argument for the simple reason that all argument on this subject presupposes it, presupposes, that is, that human language does not lose its validity when applied to God. We must speak of God in such terms as we possess or not at all. The parables of Jesus imply that there is sufficient similarity between nature, man, and God to justify the use of the first two as illustrations of the third. Is not the opening sentence of the Lord's Prayer a case of analogy?

So far we have considered Aquinas as a theist. But of course he was more than that. He was a devout Christian in a time when Christianity was confronted in Islam by its most powerful and dangerous opponent since the end of paganism in the Roman Empire. Mohammed challenged Jesus, the Koran claimed to supersede the Gospels. Where was the truth to be found as between these two rivals? The *Summa Contra Gentiles* is an attempt to answer these questions, and it seeks to establish the truth of Christianity by arguments that have only recently lost their force for us. He appeals to the O.T. prophecies as history written in advance and fulfilled in every detail by the life and work of Christ, to the miracles that accompanied the first proclamation of the faith, and to the credibility of witnesses who had only suffering and death to expect as a reward for their message. That is to say, Christianity is vindicated, not by reference to its content as a Gospel, but on the ground of external evidence.[2]

[2] In this, it should be said, he was only following in the footsteps of earlier apologists for Christianity *vis-a-vis* Islam, from John of Damascus onward.

It might seem from this that one accepts Christianity as one does a proposition in physics, because the evidence for it is convincing. That of course is not the case. One becomes a Christian by faith. How then are we to understand faith? The arguments Aquinas has set out are not sufficient to carry conviction to one brought up, say, in Islam, but they do dispose him to look favourably upon the body of Christian teaching as a whole. This then exerts over him the attraction that is inherent in it, it meets his need, opens to him a realm in which he could wish to dwell. There still remains, and always will remain, a gap between what Christianity offers and what the intellect can establish. Faith is the act by which a man closes the gap, identifying himself with what the heart affirms and reason does not deny.

CHAPTER IV   Sin and Salvation

THE specific character or, as one might put it, the *style* of a civilization turns in the last resort on the picture of man that is in the minds of those who belong to it. So much at least we have learned from Russia. Now the picture of man that largely governed the medieval mind and is still of great power wherever the influence of the Catholic Church extends, while by no means the work of Aquinas, received from him sharpness and definition. He filled in and filled out the sketch that came down to him from his predecessors. As might be expected, his conception of man is a two-story one, the substructure being classical and Aristotelian, the superstructure Biblical and Christian. Man as he came from the hands of the Creator in Paradise was constituted at once a rational and social being (the lower story) and a being capable of fellowship with God and eternal life (the upper story). The first was natural, the second supernatural, an extraordinary endowment of God's grace.

"Our first parents were established with a supernatural gift, namely, the grace of *original justice*, which rendered their reasons obedient to God, their

69

sense-powers to their reason, and their bodies to their soul".[3]

Unfortunately, that happy condition did not continue. Adam sinned, and the consequences of his sin devolved, not only on himself, but also on his descendants to the end of time. This is no legal fiction, no arbitrary punishment of the innocent for the guilty. The quotation just given goes on:

> The deed of gift was not granted to private persons, but to the ancestors of the human race for transmission to their posterity. The loss of the gift followed the same tenor; it went from them and from their descendants.

For Aquinas mankind is not a collection of individuals, it is a single organism to which individuals belong much as the limbs of the body belong to it.

> The sin of one sinner is one sin. Though executed by diverse members, it is committed by one single organism, and comes from one will.[4]

Hence all men are born without the original justice that Adam held in trust for them but lost, therefore without the power to control the senses and appetites at the behest of reason. The second and positive aspect of the injury is that each generation transmits concupiscence, random and unlawful desire, to the next. And since all participated in Adam's act, this condition of original sin constitutes mankind a guilty, as well as a weak and sinful, race.

It is clear that from so dire a condition man cannot hope to save himself. Salvation must come from God. And God acts for man's salvation by becoming incarnate in Jesus Christ. Here particularly Aquinas does but dot the i's and cross the t's of numerous theologians before him, noticeably Athanasius and others who fixed the pattern of orthodox Christology. There had been a suggestion in scholastic circles that the Incar-

---

[3] St. Thomas Aquinas: *Theological Texts,* trans. Thomas Silby, 1955, p. 121. Note that justice here = righteousness.
[4] *Ibid.,* pp. 121, 124.

nation would have taken place even had man not fallen, and some moderns have been attracted by this view. Aquinas declines to dogmatize on the subject, but is not disposed to agree. He accepted, of course, the Chalcedonian dogma that Christ is one person in two natures, human and divine, "the distinction of natures being by no means taken away by the union, but rather the property of each nature being preserved, and concurring in one person and one substance". It has to be remembered that terms like 'person' and 'nature' do not mean for him what they have come to mean for us in the light of our much larger knowledge of psychology. The same caution is even more necessary when we find Aquinas clear that there were two wills in Christ. For us, two wills in one person means, at the best, conflict, and at the worst, dissociation. Both are inconceivable from the standpoint of Aquinas.

He does not make the mistake of some theologians, both before and since, who attach value to the Incarnation or the Cross, robbing the teaching and ministry of any significance. Nevertheless, he devotes special attention to the Atonement. In his death Christ acted as a public person, not as a private one. As all men were involved in the sin of Adam, so all the faithful benefit by the passion of Christ, as members of the Church, his mystical body. But how does his death avail for them? Anselm had developed a theory according to which Christ made satisfaction for the sins of men (not, be it noted, by being *punished* in their place, but by offering to God a perfect obedience throughout his life and consummating this in his death), Abelard had represented the Cross as the supreme appeal of God's love to our hearts, winning us to penitence. Aquinas accepted both views, making the second subsidiary to the first, though he understood satisfaction as, in part at least, bearing the punishment due to sin. In his human nature Christ was an instrument of his divine nature, and so he made satisfaction for us i.e. "offered to God more than what was demanded as recompense for the sin of the entire human race". He "liberates us from the debt of punishment".[5] Offering himself for us in so great love, he wins us to love God in return,

[5] *Ibid.*, pp. 330, 334.

so that we can be forgiven and live in obedience to him henceforth.

In the next section something will be said of how all this bears upon the Church and its sacraments. Here it will be sufficient to note that the life of the redeemed in its turn has its classical substructure and its Christian superstructure. That is to say, Aquinas's ethics represent the baptism of Aristotle into Christ. The lower level is that of the cardinal virtues (prudence, justice, fortitude, temperance), the upper that of the theological (faith, hope, charity). Of course, the Christian life is not in two corresponding parts: what can be analyzed as two is in actual living one. For in according with the principle that grace does not destroy nature but fulfils, enhances, and elevates it, the cardinal virtues in the Christian are no longer merely human achievements; they are related to God and prompted and sustained by his grace. The theological virtues are beyond human power and therefore are spoken of as 'infused'. Such a term might suggest that the virtues are poured into us from outside: in which case would they be either ours or virtues? But Aquinas does not mean to imply this. "The Holy Ghost", he says, "moves the will to love, but in such a way that we are principal causes".[6] He wants, that is to say, to do justice both to God's grace and to man's freedom.

CHAPTER V   Church and Sacrament

ALL that has been said hitherto must of course be set in the context of the Church as a visible society centred upon Rome and divinely commissioned to convey God's truth to mankind by its teaching, and to create, nourish, and direct the life in grace by its sacraments. The Church was, it is true, founded by Christ: but more important for Aquinas is the fact that it continues his life. It is his mystical body, so termed "by analogy with a human physical body which performs different functions through different members".[7] One point at

[6] *Ibid.*, p. 214.
[7] *Ibid.*, p. 337.

which the analogy breaks down is that the Church includes the faithful departed as well as those who are alive and within it today. The Church is marked off from all competing societies by four features. It is one, as opposed to the divisive character of heresy. "The Church is like the Ark of Noah, outside of which nobody can be saved."[8] But the Church's unity is to be one of mutual love, not merely one of organization. It is holy as indwelt by the Holy Spirit, catholic as universal, and lasting as guaranteed by the Lord himself. The Pope is the visible head of the Church, in whom all its powers are gathered up, who convenes councils and decides what is and what is not an article of faith.

Within the saving society thus described the population of Western Europe grew up, with the single exception of the Jew; for even the heretic would in all probability have received Catholic baptism. The seven sacraments of the Church provided for the spiritual life of the individual from the cradle to the grave. In his earliest childhood he was brought to the font to receive baptism, by confirmation he was admitted to the Eucharist; if he sinned, he could be restored by penance; when he married, the priest administered another sacrament; the priest himself had received his supernatural powers in ordination. Finally, as he lay dying he would receive extreme unction. Through these sacraments the divine grace was at once symbolized and conveyed. "The sacraments of the New Law really contribute to the reception of grace."[9] Not, to be sure, that there is anything magical in the process. It must be admitted, however, that Aquinas sometimes uses language that would suggest that grace works in the sacraments like a force or a thing: it "perfects the soul's substance", we are told, "which thereby partakes of, and is likened to, the divine being".[10] He did not devote sufficient attention to the response that is needed on our side if the offer God makes in the sacrament is to be received and become effective. Faith is still with him the acceptance of the Church's teaching, not the personal trust in a gracious God it was to be for Luther.

[8] *Ibid.*, p. 341.
[9] *Ibid.*, p. 355.
[10] *Ibid.*, p. 358.

It is only possible here to glance at the treatment by Aquinas of the two main sacraments, baptism and the Eucharist. The first of these effects a profound change in the infant who receives it, so that, as the term 'christening' implies, he becomes a Christian thereby. That is to say, the guilt of original sin is washed away and the seed of a new life is implanted in the infant. Thus the whole efficacy of Christ's passion is communicated to him; he dies to sin and rises to the Christian life. Not that all the sinful nature handed down from Adam is eradicated in the water. Enough remains to make it possible for him to fall into actual sin if he yields to it, and therefore enough to make it necessary for him constantly to receive fresh supplies of grace through the other sacraments if he is to resist its solicitations. If conditions make baptism in water impossible, baptism by desire is of equal efficacy, and none doubted that martyrdom was an equivalent.

The crucial point of Catholic doctrine on the Eucharist is transubstantiation. This has played so major a part in European thought and life that it is important that those whose upbringing has prejudiced them against it, should try to understand it. Thomas works with the distinction, derived from Aristotle, between substance and accident, between that which makes a thing what it is and the properties that are ascribed to it. We say that 'Ink is fluid', and we are led to distinguish in thought between something about the ink to which the property of fluidity attaches and that property itself. We can distinguish these only in thought, but God can do so in fact. Thus

the whole substance of bread is converted into the whole substance of Christ's body, the whole substance of wine into the whole substance of his blood.

But

it is evident to the senses that all the accidents of bread and wine remain after consecration.[11]

it is therefore beside the point to say that the consecrated wafer looks like bread and tastes like bread, or that on chemical analysis it shows all the properties of

[11] *Ibid.*, p. 370.

bread. The theory provides for that in advance. Whether we agree with it or not, the doctrine is at least intellectually respectable and worthy of consideration.

Of course, Aristotle's philosophy here, as elsewhere, was enlisted in the service of the Christian faith. Aquinas did not doubt that the words of the Lord: "This is my body" must be taken literally. Nor did Luther, and his insistence on this, even while he rejected transubstantiation, was the main obstacle to a union of the German and Swiss reformations. Perhaps the Reformers might have been more disposed to look favourably on the medieval explanation of the Eucharist had it not been for the sacrificial significance that had come to be attached to it. The Mass is termed by Aquinas "the immolation of Christ" and he further defines this by speaking of it as "an image representing Christ's Passion" and as a memorial, a commemoration of it; also "through this sacrament we are made partakers of the fruit of our Lord's Passion". It is not that Calvary is supplemented by the Mass; as the Church is his body, so the sacrifice of the altar is the sacrifice of the Cross. There is no other.

There is one Christ, not many offered by Christ and us . . .

There is one body, not many, and so, wherever he is offered, the sacrifice is one and the same with his.[12]

CHAPTER VI   Political Philosophy

ONE of the most important items in the legacy of the ancient world to the medieval was the notion of law, and of law as not merely an arbitrary command of some holder of power, but as grounded in the nature of things and above all in the nature of man. The law of nature of which the Stoics spoke did not mean what the term suggests to us, the uniformities to be detected in the physical world, but something quite different, an obligation incumbent upon man as man and therefore upon all men, regardless of their origin. Aquinas car-

[12] *Ibid.*, pp. 374f.

ries his analysis of the concept of law a stage further back. He sets out from God and the eternal law, which he defines as "the idea existing in God as the principle of the universe and lying behind the governance of things". Man as a rational creature has a share in this eternal law, certain first principles that belong to it being communicated to him. This is natural law, which expresses "what is fitting and commensurate to man's very nature".[13] It includes, not only those first principles just mentioned, but also such deductions from them as commend themselves to our reason. The institution of private property is a case in point.

That private property is grounded in natural law does not mean, however, that the existing distribution of property in a society is just. It may or not be so. For societies are administered in accordance with positive law, which is laid down by the competent authority. We may note in passing that Aquinas recognizes a divinely revealed positive law, the Mosaic: his argument, though, is mainly concerned with such positive law as is of human origin. Where this emanates from the state it is called civil law, where from the Church, it is called canon law. Positive law may take up into itself precepts from natural law, as when it legislates for the stability of marriage and the family. It may defy natural law, as when—this at least is the Catholic judgment—it permits abortion or the use of contraceptives. It may apply natural law, as when it regulates the conditions on which property may be inherited. In this last case, when tested by natural law, it may be judged that the positive law in question is just or unjust. For natural law provides the criterion by which all human laws are to be assessed, and no such law is morally binding if it violates the principles of natural law.

What is the place of the state in this scheme? It is rooted in human nature because man is made for society. Aquinas agrees with Aristotle that the state has as its aim the good life for all within it, and comes into being to promote this more efficiently and more comprehensively than is possible in the simpler forms of association. His opinion on the best form of state is strikingly modern:

[13] St. Thomas Aquinas: *Philosophical Texts,* trans. Thomas Gilby, 1951, pp. 357-359.

Two points should be observed concerning the healthy constitution of a state or nation. One is that all should play a responsible part in the governing: this ensures peace, and the arrangement is liked and maintained by all. The other concerns the type of government; on this head the best arrangement for a state or government is for one to be placed in command, presiding by authority over all, while under him are others with administrative powers, yet for the rulers to belong to all because they are elected by and from all. Such is the best polity, well combined from the different strains of monarchy, since there is one at the head; of aristocracy, since many are given responsibility; and of democracy, since the rulers are chosen from and by the people.[14]

The question of private ownership and its justification has been touched on above. Perhaps it will be of interest to summarize briefly Aquinas's teaching on this point. The Fathers followed Seneca in distinguishing between the original happy state of mankind, in which all things were in common, and its present condition, in which evil has done so much injury that the institution of private property is necessary to prevent still more. Aquinas operates with a somewhat different scheme. He grants that since God is Creator and Lord of all, all things are his possession and therefore cannot be man's in an absolute sense. But he has granted to man a relative ownership, that is, the right to use and enjoy. The main ground of this is that property will be more wisely administered when some one person has a clear-cut and legally recognized interest in it, and that peace will be better preserved when the boundaries are fixed between what is mine and what is yours. "Hence private ownership is not contrary to natural law, but is an addition to it devised by human reason."[15] Such ownership, it must be stressed, is not absolute. There is a sense in which all things must still be held in common. He who has is under the obligation to meet the needs of those who have not.

We may conclude with a glance at Aquinas's position on war and peace. The medieval concept of the

14 *Ibid.*, p. 382.
15 *Ibid.*, p. 346.

just war (*justum bellum*) which has come to the front again in recent discussion received its full formulation from the great Jesuit theologians of the post-Reformation period. It stems from the attempt of the medieval Church to bridle the ferocities of kings and lords by an appeal to the Christian ethic to which they paid homage. The main conditions under which war is permissible had been sketched by Augustine, and he is followed by Aquinas, who lays down three conditions. First, war must be waged by a sovereign and not by a private person. Second, it should be entered upon solely to redress some wrong of which the other party has been guilty. Third, it should be waged with due restraint, so that the harm done is confined to what is strictly requisite if the objective of the war is to be achieved. There is for Aquinas no autonomy of the political sphere. Nor does he allow it to the economic sphere. While considerations such as those of supply and demand must enter into the fixing of wages and prices, these should be subordinate in the last resort to moral considerations. Not 'the haggling of the market' is the final court of appeal, but justice, and it is the duty of constituted authority to help determine what, in each situation, is the just price or the just wage.[16]

For further reading:

Dominican translation of *Summa Theologica and Contra Gentiles.*
M. C. D'Arcy: *Thomas Aquinas.*
F. Copleston: *Aquinas.*

[16] While usury (lending at interest) is sin, Aquinas allows interest in the case of investment (*Summa Theologica*, Dominican trans., X, pp. 336f.).

PART FIVE

LUTHER

CHAPTER I   The Background

WE who look back on the middle ages are apt to think of Thomism as reigning supreme then as it has since come to do within the Roman Church. But the thirteenth century was a time of ferment and doubt, as well as of systematic exposition and vindication of the faith. Frederick II was a contemporary of Aquinas, and this amazing man actually launched the sixth Crusade while still under a Papal ban, and concluded it by a friendly arrangement with the Sultan of Egypt! There was therefore, at least in the realm of thought, no 'medieval synthesis' that subsequently broke down. The work of Aquinas was taken up among the Dominicans, but the Franciscan tradition was a different one. Robert Grosseteste, Bishop of Lincoln and teacher at Oxford in this same century, prepared the way for modern science and the experimental method. The name of Roger Bacon is better known, and he was born some ten or twelve years before Aquinas. Nor was theology confined within the Thomist frontiers. It is of the utmost importance for an understanding of Luther and his thought to bear in mind that, as an Augustinian monk, though he knew the great *Summa* of Aquinas, he was not trained on it but on the works of William of Occam and his followers.

Occam ranks as one of the most independent spirits Oxford has ever nurtured and he was certainly the *enfant terrible* among the churchmen of his day. He began his theological studies at Oxford early in the fourteenth century, and his career thereafter was a stormy one. In the conflict between the Pope and Ludwig of Bavaria, he espoused the cause of the latter, arguing for the independence of the temporal power over against the Papacy, and advocating for the Church the form of a constitutional monarchy rather than a despotism. Theologically, he refused to cross from reason to revelation by any such bridge as that which Aquinas had laboured to construct. Only by a leap could one effect the passage. That is to say, the truths of revelation cannot be grounded in reason, they cannot even be shown to be compatible with reason. Indeed, sometimes reason would dispute them with apparently cogent arguments. But in such cases authority—and by this he meant primarily the Bible—has given us the truth, and this we must accept even against reason. Further, he reversed the relation Aquinas had established between intellect and will, and asserted the primacy of the latter. The consequences of this were serious. On the one hand, a world that is the expression of God's will rather than of his reason is one that must be investigated piece by piece and may not at any point be deduced from *a priori* principles. On the other this position introduces uncertainty into morality, since what is right and what is wrong has been fixed by God's decree, and there is no guarantee that he will not change. Might he not, for example, make falsehood a virtue and truthfulness a vice, if the only reason why they are now otherwise is that he willed it should be so?

It is clear from what has been said so far that the transition from the medieval world to the modern was a process rather than a crisis. That does deny the special place in the development that must be assigned to what we call the Renaissance, especially in its Italian form. It was in part a revival of Platonism or even of Neoplatonism, in part an awakening to secular interests and their release from domination by the Church; at once a rediscovery of the old and a movement towards the new. Pantheistic tendencies in philosophy, the new cosmology of Copernicus and Galileo, the tyrants and city-states of Italy, Machiavellianism in politics, the patronage of art by luxury-loving and wordly-minded Popes—these are some of the aspects of the Renaissance with which we are all familiar. Luther nailed his theses to the church door at Wittenberg (1517) two years before Leonardo da Vinci died and Magellan set sail to circumnavigate the globe. But this brilliant Europe was in deadly peril. Ten years later the armies of Islam were to be beaten off in the desperate defense of Vienna.

But it was the Northern Renaissance rather than the Southern that was to furnish the background for Luther's work, and in this the principal figure was Erasmus, that amazing man who, by sheer intellectual power, became the idol of students, the companion of kings, and the scourge of monks. While he refused to identify himself with the reform, it would scarcely have been possible without him, and one of the most important events in European history was the publication in 1516 of the first printed Greek New Testament, which was definitely intended to serve as the basis for translations into the vernacular. His own idea was a simple Christian philosophy, to which Cicero, the New Testament, and the Fathers would all contribute, and he wanted reform from within and without open strife. As we shall see, he was eventually persuaded to join issue with Luther. Rome rewarded him in the end by placing his writings on the Index.

Rightly to appreciate Luther and his success, one has to bear in mind, not only the Renaissance and the work of Erasmus, but also a growing resentment on the part of Germans against a Papacy that was always Italian and not always respectable. What provoked Luther to put his theology into overt action—though of course he had no intention at this stage of breaking with the Papacy—was the crass commercialism of the sale of indulgences by Tetzel. Erasmus had satirized the cunning of those who sold, and the gullibility of those who bought these, and the Elector of Saxony, later to stand before the world as Luther's staunch protector, refused to allow the traffic in his dominions. The purpose of the traffic was to embellish St. Peter's, that monument to the glory of the Renaissance Popes rather than of God. Thousands who were not competent to follow a theological argument rallied to a German who had dared to challenge a regime that seemed to think of Germany only to exploit it and refused reform lest vested interests suffer.

Justification by Faith

As a historical phenomenon, the Reformation needs to be studied from several angles, and a total presentation would require that account be taken of social, political, and economic factors. Yet it would be the gravest of misjudgments to suppose that the religious element could be assigned any but the most important place. Nor can the achievement of Luther be understood unless it be borne in mind that he was an intensely religious personality, with a passion for God and for a right relation to him. For this he entered the monastery against his father's wishes, because it seemed to him that there only could he find peace with God and assurance of salvation. When he was ordained priest, he was almost overwhelmed with the awful responsibility as, in his first Mass, he pronounced the tremendous words by which he, a mortal man, could change the bread and wine into the body and blood of the Lord. He was not a man to be satisfied with half-measures; having vowed himself to God's service, he was resolved to bring to him his all. When he found that his best efforts ended in failure, he suffered the torments of a conscience in distress, and the question that haunted him was: How can I find a gracious God?

The trials to which Luther was subjected in the monastery arose out of the discipline of the medieval church and the theology in which he had been trained. This was the theology of Gabriel Biel, a disciple of Occam. According to Biel, the sacrament of penance availed for the forgiveness of sins only if the recipient came to it duly prepared by love of God and full penitence. He must, and could, reach this condition himself, and then the sacrament would infuse the necessary grace for pardon and new life. But Luther found it quite impossible to reach either penitence or the love of God: it was useless to say that forgiveness was waiting for him, when it was always beyond his reach. He knew, of course, that a confessor trained in this theology would in fact be less severe; he would work with the principle that if we do what is in our power,

God will surely supply the rest. But how could he be sure that he had done what was in his power? A suggestion of this kind was no comfort for a man with his passion for the absolute; his sense of the utter holiness of God as a continual condemnation even of his best and most earnest efforts. He read that "the righteousness ('justice' in the Vulgate) of God" is revealed in the Gospel (Rom. i. 16f.) and trembled as he thought what it meant to come under that righteousness.

One of his superiors, Staupitz by name, was able to help him to some extent by drawing on an older tradition derived from Augustine and preserved in part in Aquinas, according to which God's grace does not wait upon our desert. But even his best advisers left untouched the dread words in Paul; God's righteousness became almost hateful in Luther's eyes and he longed to know how he might find mercy in God rather than wrath. Light came to him in the Black Tower of Wittenberg as he wrestled with Paul over this point. He saw in a flash that, for Paul, God's righteousness is not opposed to his mercy; it is its consummation. God's righteousness is not what he demands from men, but what he gives to them. It is his acceptance of them, not because they have deserved it, but out of his own goodness. This is the doctrine of justification by faith that was Luther's great discovery or, as he would say, his rediscovery of the Gospel. It is most simply presented in the parable of the Pharisee and the publican. He who seeks to earn God's acceptance by his moral and religious achievements only ends in pride and self-satisfaction, coupled with a censorious attitude towards his fellows. God is to be found as we surrender all claims upon him and receive from him an entirely undeserved mercy.

What made this new, illuminating, and saving interpretation of Paul possible was the apprehension of God in Christ, and this also was derived from Paul. In Christ God has opened to us his heart of love, in Christ he has sought out and saved the lost. The initiative was taken by God, and the place where he did this was Calvary. There God's justice and mercy were one, for Christ died for our sins as we deserved to die because God wished us to live and not to die. And this incredible mercy is grasped by faith. Faith is the abandonment of oneself to God in Christ. The paradox is that out of the renunciation of our efforts to commend ourselves to God by faultless obedience there issues an obedience beyond anything that was possible hitherto. For, certain as Luther was that faith *alone* justifies—which is another way of saying that Christ alone does—he was equally certain that it could never *be alone,* and it must always be active in love.

This central principle of the Reformation has so often been misrepresented that we must linger over it awhile. Roman Catholic objections to it are irrelevant. For Catholic theology includes under justification the whole development of the Christian life and regards faith as the acceptance of Christian doctrine from the Church. Luther did not teach *such* justification by *such* faith! Nor is the later language of an imputed righteousness that leaves the actual condition of the recipient untouched to be carried back to Luther. For him, the justified person is not merely *declared* righteous, he *becomes* such. For he is incorporated by faith in Christ and so begins to be transformed into his likeness. Luther does not think there are two paths to righteousness, one by effort and the other by faith; the only righteousness open to man in this world is the humble recognition of one's unrighteousness, gratitude for an unmerited mercy, loyalty to Christ who gave himself to death for our sakes, and love towards all men, since all share the curse of sin and need the blessing of forgiveness. And moral effort is more successful when it ceases to be the means by which we earn God's favour and becomes our response to it as a free gift.

CHAPTER III   God Hidden and Revealed

THIS problem of the guilty conscience, which shook Luther to the very centre of his being and as a result gravely endangered so stable and venerable an institution as the medieval Church, may well seem to many an artificial one. They would take God's goodness for granted or at least they would assume that he will not press his demands on us beyond our powers, so that there is no occasion for anxiety. But Luther took both the moral life and his relation to God too seriously to think in those terms. There was no doubt a strong strain of pessimism in Luther, and the language he sometimes used about man's sinfulness appears exaggerated from our point of view. But both are due to the fact that he is not passing a judgment, either on himself or on man, from the everyday standpoint, but from that of God's awful holiness. Before this

> we are clean overwhelmed and drowned in sins. Whatsoever is in our will is evil; whatsoever is in our understanding is error. Wherefore *in matters pertaining* to God man hath nothing but darkness, errors, malice, and perverseness both of will and understanding.[1]

What I have called Luther's passion for the absolute led him to crave for certainty, for the assurance that God in Christ had been gracious to him personally. And he won through to this, and to the conviction also that he had a prophetic mission, that he was a man raised up by God to purify the Church in the last days. Much in him is strange to our way of thinking, especially the grim realism with which he wrestled with devils and the bold expostulation of his prayers. He did not think of himself as founding a church that would last for centuries, but as standing for God in a day when Antichrist was raging, the Turk was marching from victory to victory, sin was on the increase, and the Lord's return could not be far away. He wrote:

> "The world runs and hastens so diligently to its end that it often occurs to me that the last day will break before we can completely turn the Holy Scriptures into German." [2]

What does appeal to us is that this amazing confidence and sense of mission was maintained in face of constant doubt and trial. It was not merely that he was conscious of his human weaknesses; God was for him

[1] *A Commentary on St. Paul's Epistle to the Galatians,* 1953, pp. 175f. Italics not in the original.

[2] H. T. Kerr: *A Compend of Luther's Theology,* 1943, p. 245.

at once the source of anxiety and the deliverance from it.

This brings us to the theme of the hidden God (*Deus absconditus*) and the revealed God (*Deus revelatus*). It is not that these are two different Gods, they are one and the same, and salvation lies in grasping their unity. This unity in its turn is made possible only in Christ. Luther's thinking is at once theocentric and Christocentric. Let us glance at three instances of the opposition and reconciliation of these two aspects in one God.

The first is that of *law* and *Gospel,* which carries with it that of *wrath* and *mercy.* God speaks to us with two voices, in condemnation from Sinai and in forgiveness from Calvary. His wrath is as much a reality as his mercy. He is the sentence of death upon us as well as the gift of eternal life. Nor are these two opposed. For his forgiveness brings peace of conscience only because it is the expression of absolute holiness. God kills that he may restore to life, sends us down into the hell of self-condemnation and the fear of judgment that he may raise us from it to the heaven that is the light of his countenance. How he does this we see in Christ. Faith discerns in Christ how the hidden God from whom we shrink in terror is at the same time the revealed God who invites us to draw near.

In one sense therefore the hidden God is to be equated with *God apart from Christ* and the revealed God with *God in Christ.* Hence Luther's criticism of natural theology. The scholastic discussion of God's essence and attributes is the invasion by man of a territory God has reserved for himself: he wills to be known by us as he has revealed himself in Jesus Christ, the incarnate Word, and so only can he be known. All knowledge of God is worthless that is not personal and practical.

We should note that there are two ways of believing. One way is to believe about God, as I do when I believe that what is said about God, is true; just as I do when I believe what is said about the Turk, the devil or hell. This faith is knowledge or observation rather than faith. The other way is to believe in God, as I do when I not only believe that what is said about him is true, but put my trust in him, surrender myself to him and make bold to deal with him, believing without doubt that he will be to me and do to me just what is said of him.[3]

But even in Christ we have both aspects of God. There it is indeed that we are able to perceive as nowhere else the identity of the hidden God and the revealed God. In a tremendous passage commenting on Gal. iii, 13, Luther imagines God sending his Son into the world, saying to him: "Be thou David the adulterer, Saul the blasphemer, etc.", and all out of love for mankind. Calvary is the point at which he whom God abandons is at the same time he whom he loves.

Finally, the hidden God is seen in the grim reality of *predestination*, the revealed God in the open proclamation of *the Gospel*. Luther joined issue with Erasmus over the freedom of the will, a new Augustine facing a second and more learned Pelagius. Luther's extremism is stamped on every page of his *Bondage of the Will*. He reduces man to utter helplessness, making of him a beast that now God, now Satan mounts. But his interest, as always, is practical and religious. Wrongly, no doubt, he thinks that faith is endangered and answers to prayer uncertain if any human agency is allowed power alongside God. His concern is with the utter reliability of God as the ground of our salvation. Therefore while allowing full weight to the will of God that determines our destiny apart from any merit of ours, he insists that this is not to be preached from the pulpit. The God who is to be offered to men is the Father whose limitless mercy has come to us in Christ.

CHAPTER IV Let God be God

THERE is a popular misunderstanding of Luther that would see in him the champion of a purely subjective religion, one that makes not only the conscience, but

[3] *The Works of Martin Luther*, Philadelphia edition, II, p. 368.

even the feelings of the individual a final court of appeal. No doubt there have been tendencies of this kind within Lutheranism, but the reformer himself was of a much more robust and virile type. He put his trust at no point in man but always in God. P. S. Watson has expressed this well by giving his study of Luther the title *Let God be God*. We consider briefly some of the points at which Luther felt it necessary to contend for the honour of God.

(i) This was clearly the issue in the controversy over indulgences out of which the Reformation sprang. The sale of indulgences was a corrupt practice that developed gradually out of what in the first instance was a quite restricted and carefully guarded theory of the Church's power to absolve. The Ninety-five Theses do not repudiate the theory, but only the abuses.

> Christians are to be taught that the Pope's pardons are useful, if they do not put their trust in them; but altogether harmful, *if through them they lose their fear of God*.[4]

(ii) The objection to indulgences was to any sale of that grace of God that is given freely to all in Christ. As such, it was one instance of something that often takes a less exceptionable form, the effort to secure one's salvation by works, to commend oneself to God by moral achievement or the performance of religious duties. The more overt forms of this were the erection and endowment of churches, pilgrimages to Rome or to the shrine of some saint, the recitation of prayers, and so on. It is against these that Luther particularly directs his attack, and the gravamen of his charge is that they are self-chosen. Men give to God what *they* wish to give, whereas they should be content with humble obedience to what *he* commands. Hence the *Treatise on Good Works* opens with the sentence:

> We ought first to know that there are no good works except those which God has commanded, even as there is no sin except that which God has forbidden. Therefore whoever wishes to know and to do good works needs nothing else than to know God's commandments.[5]

[4] *Works*, I, p. 34. Italics not in the original.
[5] *Works*, I, p. 187.

Of course, when we set ourselves to keep God's commandments, we are exposed to the temptation of self-righteousness in a less overt, but as deadly form. Pride, self-satisfaction, the heart turned in upon itself—these are signs that we are trying to raise ourselves to God when we should be receiving God who comes down to us in Christ.

(iii) It was on this ground also that Luther passed, under the pressure of events, from his original appeal to the Pope to defend the Church's honour against those who wrongly cited his authority to his final repudiation of the Pope as Antichrist. For what is the mark of Antichrist? Is it not that "he sitteth in the temple of God, setting himself forth as God" (2 Thess. ii, 4)? In Luther's time, it was still an open question among the theologians whether final authority in the Church rested with the Pope or with a General Council, and he was at first disposed to think that, if the Pope refused to hear God's word through him, a Council would set the affairs of the Church in order. He was driven, however, to admit that a Council might err and that Scripture was the ultimate court of appeal. When in 1520 he took the drastic step of publicly committing to the flames the Papal bull of excommunication he acted on the conviction he had by then reached, that the Pope was not in fact the Vicar of Christ but his supreme and last enemy, the man who usurped for himself the honour due to God alone.

(iv) The Mass was the centre of medieval piety, though it must always be borne in mind that the fear inspired by belief in transubstantiation was such that the laity, when attending Mass, usually did so as spectators and only very rarely as communicants. A quotation from a modern writer will show how inevitable was Luther's opposition to the Mass.

Hence you cannot but perceive the incredible cogency of the Mass. It is a gift that God cannot resist: the priest, and the layman too, since there is a solidarity between them, and the priest is but the instrumental cause of the offering of Mass, have omnipotence in their hands.[6]

[6] C. C. Martindale: *The Faith of the Roman Church*, 1950, p. 87.

Especially repugnant was the offering of Mass as a sacrifice for the benefit of the departed, since here again a man did something that pleased *him*, and did it to establish a claim on God. He gave "a gift that God cannot resist"! What blasphemy in Luther's eyes!

(v) Finally, we come to Luther's opposition to the Anabaptists, one of the most regrettable features in his life. Contemporary Lutheran theologians are disposed to revise the reformer's judgment on the radical Protestantism of the time, and to urge that the 'Church' should be willing to learn from the 'sect' as it has not done in the past. What Luther shrank from was a translation of the Gospel as he preached it into the language of social revolution, and he was disposed—not unnaturally—to identify all the Anabaptists with that one group of them which resorted to violence in the effort to realize a Christian society. Whereas for the Anabaptists life took precedence of doctrine, these for Luther stood in reverse order.[7] That is to say, for Luther the Gospel was the message of God's forgiving grace to sinful man, and when Carlstadt suggested that this was but *one item* in the total Gospel, he feared that once again some human 'work' was being given the value that belongs to God alone. Hence his insistence that perfection is not within our reach here below, to the end of our days we shall be sinners wholly dependent upon God. Nothing, be it ecclesiastical authority or individual piety and morality, must be allowed to contract by one inch the awful gulf between God's holiness and man's sin.[8]

---

[7] This important difference has been demonstrated and its significance discussed in K. G. Steck: *Luther und die Schwärmer*, 1955.

[8] For Luther's emphasis on baptism as an objective guarantee, see *Works*, I, p. 63. "We must hold boldly and fearlessly to our baptism, and hold it up against all sins and terrors of conscience, and humbly say, 'I know full well that I have not a single work which is pure, but I am baptized, and through my baptism God, who cannot lie, has bound himself in a covenant with me, not to count my sin against me, but to slay it and blot it out'."

CHAPTER V

Freedom in God

OF one thing Luther was convinced to the end of his days, that all the goodness, the strength, and the security man can hope for in this world are to be found in God, and in him alone. When Schleiermacher found the essence of religion in the feeling of absolute dependence, he was true to Luther inasmuch as he stressed man's dependence on God, untrue to him as he made this a feeling rather than an objective fact. But this dependence on God, as Luther understood it, was the source of all man's independence and freedom. One of the best known of his writings is the *Treatise of Christian Liberty,* and its message is summarized in two propositions on the first page:

A Christian man is a perfectly free lord of all, subject to none.
A Christian man is a perfectly dutiful servant of all, subject to all.[9]

The link that joins together these two truths is faith. This sets us free from the anxious effort to commend ourselves to God, so that, having been forgiven and received by his undeserved mercy, we can henceforth go out in love and service towards all men. We do not have to scrape and save up for ourselves, but to employ in deeds of love the capital God has invested in us in Christ.

One aspect of this freedom has been of the utmost historical importance. The medieval church worked with the distinction between the commandments that are obligatory on all Christians and the counsels of perfection some may voluntarily take upon themselves. Foremost among the latter were celibacy and poverty. It is difficult to see how some such distinction can be avoided; but it is not necessary to go on, as the medieval church did, to grade celibacy as more pleasing to God than marriage, or to suppose that the fulfilment of these

[9] *Works,* II p. 312.

counsels of perfection constitutes a merit. Luther's action in marrying an ex-nun was intended as symbolic. He repudiated for himself and the movement at the head of which he stood the notion that the 'religious' life is that of priest and monk. The religious life, he urged, is not a special vocation that a few take upon themselves; it is the ordinary life lived in and with Christ to which all who bear his name are called. The concept of 'vocation' was thus applied to forms of life that had previously been stamped as 'secular'. The Christian is one who seeks no special station but does all, where he now is, to the glory of God.

This concept of vocation has become secularized in our time, so that the term is used of the teacher and the minister, but not of the postman and the engine-driver. We have indeed to consider how far the concept of Christian vocation can be applied to a society in which many a man is reconciled to his job only by his salary-check. A similar fate has overtaken the principle of the priesthood of all believers. This was meant as another application of Christian liberty. The distinction between the secular and the religious life was to be obliterated by raising the former up to the latter. He is not a priest who stands between his fellows and God, but he who brings his fellows to God, and in that sense all Christians are priests. The principle has come to be understood in purely negative fashion, as the repudiation of any human intermediary between man and God. It should be taken rather in a positive sense, as the opportunity and obligation of every Christian to share in the life of the Church by making God real to his fellows.

> A Christian man lives not in himself, but in Christ and in his neighbour. Otherwise he is not a Christian.
> Each should become as it were a Christ to the other, that we may be Christs to one another and Christ may be the same in all.[10]

The liberty of the Christian was maintained fear-lessly by Luther over against the Papacy. Whether it was adequately maintained against the state is a question that will be considered in the next section.

[10] *Works*, II pp. 338, 342.

But how, we must ask, did this liberty fare when confronted with the Bible? Is it correct to charge Luther with delivering the human mind from an infallible Church only to surrender it to an infallible book? My own answer to that question would be: Yes and No. That is to say, Luther's attitude to the Bible was a complex one. There were times when he seemed fettered by the mere letter, but at others he operated with an amazing freedom. The former attitude was exemplified in the Marburg Colloquy of 1529, at which the attempt to bring together the German and Swiss wings of the Reformation broke down, ostensibly at least, because Luther would not tolerate any but a literal interpretation of the words "This is My Body".[11]

On the other hand, Luther's description of James as an "epistle of straw" is well known. His final judgment on the book is less drastic. He cannot consider it the work of an apostle, but finds "many good sayings" in it. It therefore "need not be counted among the chief books, which are to lay the foundation of faith". What is more important than this somewhat superficial criticism of the book is the statement that

> What does not teach Christ is not apostolic, even though St. Peter or Paul taught it; again, what preaches Christ would be apostolic, even though Judas, Annas, Pilate and Herod did it.[12]

If we overlook for the moment the fact that Luther passes too easily from an estimate of the book's spiritual value to a conclusion as to its authorship, we cannot but agree with him. The purpose of the Bible as it has come down to us within the Christian community is to communicate Christ to us. Its authority lies solely in its ability to do that. The Gospel is the criterion by which the Bible itself must be judged. This, of course, is not a solution of the problem of Scriptural authority; but it shows the lines along which such a solution is to be looked for.

[11] He rejected transubstantiation, substituting for it what some would consider a yet more recondite theory, that of consubstantiation, according to which the Body of Christ is present 'in, with, and under' the bread. This owes not a little to Occam, whose influence on Luther is again to be seen here.

[12] *Ibid.*, VI, pp. 478f.

EVERYTHING that has been said so far goes to show that at the heart of Luther's thinking and implicit in his central principle of justification by faith there was a tension or, if we prefer so to call it, a dualism. The Christian is set free by God's grace from all commandments and ordinances of men and work-righteousness of his own yet, since he will continue a sinner to his dying day, there is need, not only that sin be forgiven, but also that it be curbed. This dualism meets us both in Luther's conception of the Church and in his view of the State. Writing in 1526 on the first of these, he outlined as meeting his wishes and as conforming to the Gospel, a type of Church order that is virtually that of Congregationalism. The Church would be composed of avowed Christians whose names would be entered on a list and who would meet as a fellowship for prayer, mutual edification, and the practice of charity. This would exist alongside the public worship that would cater for all and sundry, and would not assume a high standard in those who took part in it.[13]

Why then did the Churches that actually arose out of the Reformation not adopt this Congregational pattern? One must go further back and inquire why Luther himself made no effort to act on his ideal. He himself gives us the answer, in one of those sentences that derive all their force from the 'if' with which they open: "If one had the people and persons who wanted to be Christians in fact, the rules and regulations could easily be supplied".[14] There is not sufficient material for the creation of a community of openly committed disciples; one must be content indefinitely with the great institutional church that caters for the mass that only half wants to hear the Gospel. Another factor making for hesitation was the fear that the Anabaptists, in their effort to bring into being such a community, would not stop there but would go on to agitate for radical

[13] Ibid., VI, pp. 172f.
[14] Ibid., VI, p. 173.

social changes (that is, for changes Luther considered radical, though often very mild by our standards). Also, Luther was immensely indebted to the princes who gave him protection and support, and his principle of the priesthood of the laity made it natural for him to appeal to them to undertake the reforms that ecclesiastical authority refused even to consider. Hence the creation of territorial churches under the supervision of the ruler instead of Christian fellowships as originally envisaged.

If it is permissible to speak of tension in Luther's conception of the Church, dualism is clearly involved in his treatment of the Church-State problem: God

> has established two kinds of government among men. The one is spiritual; it has no sword, but it has the Word, by means of which men are to become good and righteous, so that with this righteousness they may attain everlasting life. This righteousness he administers through the Word, which he has committed to the preachers. The other is worldly government, through the sword, which aims to keep peace among men, and this he rewards with temporal blessing. For he gives to rulers so much property, honour and power, to be possessed by them above others, in order that they may serve him by administering this righteousness. Thus God himself is the founder, lord, master, protector and rewarder of both kinds of righteousness. There is no human ordinance or authority in either, but each is altogether a divine thing.[15]

We may say that God's primary will is that revealed in the Gospel, where he calls on men to live in love with all, to accept cheerfully the spoiling of their goods, to endure evil patiently, and to forgive their enemies, dismissing all thought of revenge. But since the mass of men clearly do not intend to obey this primary will, he brings into play his secondary will, by which through the instrumentality of the state he curbs their selfish and destructive impulses, creates a measure of peace and security, and gives opportunity for the Gospel to be preached and to win some at least to accept it. This is the famous doctrine of the Two

15 *Ibid.*, V, p. 39.

Realms that has been so sadly misunderstood, even to the extent of holding Luther responsible for Hitler. He did not sanction Machiavellianism, he did not make the State a law unto itself, he did not exempt any man, not even the ruler and the magistrate, from obedience to Christ's law of love. But he did teach that the person who is responsible for the government of a society composed largely of nominal Christians cannot always perform the duties of love as he would were he, as a committed Christian, in a face-to-face relation with others equally committed.

This is not to deny that Luther expressed himself on this point somewhat unguardedly or that the inferences drawn from his teaching have sometimes been unfortunate in the extreme or that he helped to perpetuate in Germany a type of society in which the subject had at all times to obey the ruler. We who live in a democratic society must look elsewhere for direction, though nothing will excuse us from facing the fundamental problem he raised. Granted that all would be well did we follow the Sermon on the Mount, what is the statesman to do now in a society that, with negligible exceptions, refuses to do anything of the kind?

For further reading:

Translations in Philadelphia edition, Library of Christian Classics, etc.
P. S. Watson: *Let God be God.*
G. Rupp: *The Righteousness of God.*
G. W. Forel: *Faith Active in Love.*

PART SIX

DESCARTES

CHAPTER I Background

LUTHER died in 1546, two months before the defeat in battle of the German Protestant princes and the temporary eclipse of their cause. Fortunately for the Reformation, an even doughtier champion had arisen by that time, the Frenchman John Calvin, who created in Geneva what H. A. L. Fisher calls "a Protestant Sparta" and made it a centre of propaganda for Western Europe. The stern Calvinist creed was to produce a race of giants, John Knox in Scotland, William the Silent in the Low Countries, and Oliver Cromwell in England. These were men who, humbly acknowledging themselves to be but clay in the hands of the Potter, dealt with their time as though it were shapeless clay for them to mould. One rebuked to her face a proud and fascinating queen, another challenged an empire in the name of freedom, and a third sent a king to the block. A passion for education was one of their characteristics and many a centre of learning, from Geneva to the New World, derived its impetus from Calvin and his masterpiece, *Institutes of the Christian Religion*.

A militant Protestantism clashed with a militant Catholicism. The Society of Jesus was recovering whole provinces for the ancient faith. A Spanish soldier turned devotee, Ignatius Loyola, fired a few companions with his ardour, and in 1540 obtained from Pope Paul III a bull establishing his new order. This was in part effect and in part cause of a new spirit that was aboard in the Church, the spirit of reform from within. It was at last becoming as clear to cardinals and bishops as it had long been clear to the common man, that the Church must put her house in order if she was to retain her place in the public life of Europe.

97

The Council of Trent dealt with the theological issues, affirming the faith and anathematizing heresy. Popes took their duties so seriously as to live an ascetic life even in the private apartments of the Vatican. The special contribution of the Jesuits to the Counter-Reformation, if we may leave out of account their role in politics, was in education. Schools and colleges sprang up staffed by Jesuits and giving the best training available. Descartes, whom we have been accustomed to regard as a pioneer of modern thought, was a pupil of the Jesuits.

The two influences spoken of thus far were religious. Much more important in the long run were the secular forces at work. A new view of the world was taking shape in men's minds. Modern science arose from the fusion of experiment and mathematics. In the name of the first, a few bold thinkers broke with authority and went out in search of facts. By means of the second they were able to master and order those facts. 'The Copernican revolution' took place when it was suggested that by taking the sun instead of the earth as the centre of the physical universe one could produce a far simpler scheme than that of Aristotle and his successors. By the beginning of the seventeenth century, the telescope had set the human eye raging over a territory as new and as rich in wonders as that on which Columbus set foot in 1492. The old assertion that the heavenly bodies are of a different stuff from that of which the earth is made had become untenable. But it was not so much that traditional opinions were refuted: men experienced an immense enlargement of their horizon; they breathed a new atmosphere. Wonder, we are told, was the beginning of philosophy, and wonder had returned.

If this were the place for a survey of scientific advance during the seventeenth century, something would have to be said of William Harvey and his discovery of the circulation of the blood, a challenge to accepted views if ever there was one. His *De Motu Cordium* was published in 1628. We are concerned rather with the application of mathematics to observed natural phenomena. Johann Kepler (1571-1630) was devout almost, by our standards, to the point of superstition, but his three laws of planetary motion mark the passage from a mystical quest for the harmony of

98

the spheres to that "worship of numerical patterns, of mathematical relations as such",[1] that forms his permanent legacy to the Western mind. He saw in mathematics the key to a satisfactory account of the physical universe, and he envisaged the process by which the cause of things, the reason why they are as they are, is to be reached. Let what is observed be reduced to quantitative terms, let measurement be made ever more exact, and let ever more inclusive generalizations be formed. The vision of a system of knowledge in which all other relations are reduced to mathematical ones had already dawned upon Kepler. It continues to this day to be the dream of some scientists and the working hypothesis of more.

What did this mean for those who took it, so to speak, into their bones? It meant that the everyday world began to take on a quite new character. Reality lay in what could be measured. The rest was but appearance. It was obviously not appearance in the sense of being mere illusion, a dream. It formed the setting of the scientist's life once he left his laboratory for a country walk or even sat down to a meal. The qualitative aspect of things, their colour, taste, and smell had to be accounted for. The suggestion was that all this was subjective, read into things by us, there because *put there,* so to speak. An orange then *is* of a certain size, shape, and weight, for these primary qualities, as we may call them, are measurable and so *really* there. But its red colour and sweet taste are secondary qualities, sensations produced in us by the impact on us of the primary ones. They are how it *appears* to us.

I think that these tastes, odours, colours, etc., on the side of the object in which they seem to exist, are nothing else than mere names, but hold their residence solely in the sensitive body; so that if the animal were removed, every such quality would be abolished and annihilated.[2]

Is the reader revolted by this, or has he always thought so?

[1] Herbert Butterfield: *The Origins of Modern Science* 1300-1800, 1949, p. 59.
[2] Galileo, quoted in E. A. Burtt: *The Metaphysical Foundations of Modern Physical Science,* 1925, p. 75.

CHAPTER II

I Think, Therefore I Am

PERHAPS the best point at which to begin an exposition of Descartes' thought is his experiment in doubt. In an age of merchant venturers, he resolved to set out on his own voyage of discovery, this time in the inner world. He would find truth. For this, he would leave the familiar landmarks behind, forsake the harbours where others lay at ease, and find a way across the trackless ocean. In other words, he would doubt all accepted opinions in the hope of finding one day a truth that was beyond question. Universal doubt was to be the means of discovering truth.

> I must once and for all, and by a deliberate effort, rid myself of all those opinions to which I have hitherto given credence, starting entirely anew, and building from the foundations up.[3]

Of course, one must live while conducting so drastic an experiment. So, for all practical purposes, he would accept the laws and customs of his country and the teaching of the Church as a guide to life. Of all else, he would empty his mind and see what remained.

It will be recalled that Augustine made much the same experiment, and it it hardly likely that Descartes was ignorant of this. (His attention was called to it by a correspondent.) There was of course one great difference between the two cases. Descartes was not as earnest in his doubt as Augustine was. He did not stake his whole being on it. But what of the experiment? How did it turn out? Was everything dissolved in uncertainty in the course of it? Not at all. For he who doubts is certain of at least one thing, that he is doubting. And it is self-evident that what doubts exist. *Cogito, ergo sum.* I think, therefore I am. But let us hear Descartes himself:

> While we thus reject all of which we can entertain

[3] Norman Kemp Smith: *Descartes' Philosophical Writings,* 1952, p. 196.

the smallest doubt, and even imagine that it is false, we easily indeed suppose that there is neither God, nor sky, nor bodies, and that we ourselves even have neither hands nor feet, nor, finally a body; but we cannot in the same way suppose that we are not while we doubt of the truth of these things; for there is a repugnance in conceiving that what thinks does not exist at the very time when it thinks. Accordingly, the knowledge, *I think, therefore I am,* is the first and most certain that occurs to one who philosophizes orderly.[4]

This is more than a train of thought in the mind of a French philosopher of the early seventeenth century. It registers a change in the outlook of Western man. Henceforth he is to look for the source of certainty in himself. We go on to ask if this is all that escapes the corrosion of doubt. At first it would appear that this is the case, for even the common assumptions of daily life are open to dispute. Is there, for example, an external world? Our senses tell us that there is and inform us in some detail of its character. But have not the senses often deceived us? Our sight tells us that the stick in the pool is bent, but we know that it is straight. How distinguish illusions from knowledge? We think to save ourselves by appealing to the propositions of mathematics as either self-evident or deduced from what is self-evident. That 'twice two makes four' is surely beyond dispute. But is it? That we *must* think in this way is clear. But suppose we are so made that we must think thus, but think mistakenly in so doing? What if what I think is one thing and what actually is another, and never the twain shall meet? Descartes puts it in mythological language:

I am supposing that there exists a very powerful, and if I may so speak, malignant being, who employs all his powers and skill in deceiving me.[5]

How is such a doubt to be quelled? A remedy for it will have to be found within the human mind, since we

---

[4] Descartes: *A Discourse on Method,* Everyman's Library, p. 167. The quotation is actually from *The Principles of Philosophy.*

[5] Smith: *Op. cit.,* p. 204.

have as yet no certainty save that of the proposition
I think, therefore I am. He first establishes that he is a
"thinking thing", by which he means

a thing that doubts, understands, affirms, denies, wills,
abstains from willing, that also can be aware of images
and sensations.[6]

Then, looking through the contents of the mind, the
ideas it has because it is human and not because it
belongs to this or that person, he finds one that stands
out above the rest. It is that of God. Where did it come?
Not from ourselves, for we are finite and so cannot
conceive of the infinite out of our own resources. Indeed, we should not know we were finite did we not
somehow have access to the infinite as the standard by
which we measure ourselves and find we fall short. The
idea must therefore come (*a*) from a source outside ourselves and (*b*) from a source that is adequate to account
for it. In other words, the only satisfactory explanation
of the idea of God in our mind is that God himself has
given it to us.

This is one way in which Descartes claims to prove
God's existence. What has he gained thereby? He has
thrown off the awful fear that he might be the victim of
some gigantic trick. He is not in the hands of a malignant demon but in those of a good and all-wise God.
All therefore that was in danger before is now secure.
Because God is, and is utterly true, we can have confidence that our senses do not lie when they tell us about
the external world. We can have confidence too in the
truths of mathematics. Of course, this does not mean
that we are infallible; since we are finite we are liable
to err. How error arises on Descartes' presuppositions
we shall see later. Meanwhile, let it be observed that
something momentous has happened. God has been
found useful to man. Man has, so to speak, the initial
capital of certainty within himself, but it bears no interest there. God enables him to invest it in the knowledge and mastery of the world around him.

[6] *Ibid.*, p. 206.

Mind and Body

THE certainty that accrues from the principle *I think, therefore I am* is absolute because it is restricted in application. It attaches only to myself as conscious. Indeed, some would say that Descartes has no right to speak of the 'self' at all, that he should have confined himself to some such statement as that 'thinking goes on, therefore whatever it is that thinks exists'. A point of language is here involved. In Latin the subject *Ego* is not made explicit, but is implied by the form of the verb *cogito*. In French, as in English, the subject must be made explicit. Let us allow, however, that Descartes may speak of the self. What is its relation to the body? Sometimes we come near to identifying the body with the self, as when it is injured and we complain of what has been done to *us*. On the other hand, we sometimes distinguish the two so sharply as to say with Socrates that he who destroys our bodies will find that he cannot touch *us*. Once we begin to consider what the self is in terms of the body we thus become confused and uncertain. If however we shred out of the experience of self all that does not certainly belong to it, we are left with consciousness.

> Simply from knowing that I exist, and that, meantime, I do not observe any other thing as evidently pertaining to my nature, i.e., to my essence, except this only, that I am a thinking thing, I rightly conclude that my essence consists in this alone, that I am a thinking thing (i.e. a substance, the whole nature or essence of which consists in thinking).[7]

What of the body then? It belongs now to what remains when the mind has been withdrawn, to the material world. What constitutes the essential characteristic of the material world, as thinking does of the physical? Descartes answers that it is extension. He takes the case of a piece of wax. I can describe its taste, smell,

[7] *Ibid.*, p. 254.

colour etc., all that have been spoken of as secondary qualities. But put the wax before the fire and watch it melt. All these and other properties undergo a change. Yet the wax is still there, as all will allow. And we can only describe it, now that all that does not belong to its essence has been withdrawn from it in thought, as "a something extended, flexible and movable".[8] In the last resort, what constitutes the wax—and this will apply to everything material—is

> the determinable, though not uniquely determined, character of being spatially extended. It is the capacity to assume, under certain and different conditions, this or that determinate size and this or that determinate shape, and, further, the capacity to move, when caused, and so to occupy different places at different times or to have its parts differently arranged at different moments.[9]

As he develops his account of matter, Descartes concentrates on extension, while taking motion for granted. The net result of the discussion thus far is that the world of our experience falls into two parts. On our side of the line we have the numerous human selves that are constituted by thought, and on the other the numerous material objects that are constituted by extension.

> Of every substance there is one principal attribute, as thinking of the mind, extension of the body. . . . Extension in length, breadth, and depth, constitutes the nature of corporeal substance; and thought the nature of thinking substance. . . . Thus we may easily have two clear and distinct notions or ideas, the one of created substance, which thinks, the other of corporeal substance, provided we carefully distinguish all the attributes of thought from those of extension.[10]

Over such a world the flag of mathematics could be run up at once and flown triumphantly. The material world is handed over to it, and, as the instance of the

[8] Everyman's Library, p. 91.
[9] S. V. Keeling: *Descartes,* 1934, p. 113.
[10] Everyman's Library, pp. 185f.

wax shows, only what is measurable and calculable gives reality, the rest is what appears so to us. A mechanical account of nature now becomes possible. And what of consciousness? It is the ghost that hovers—where? over the machine or in it? The body of man, we are expressly told, "is nothing but a statue or machine made of earth".[11]

Logically, all this would seem to imply that mind and body are so disparate that any action of one upon the other would be quite impossible. In fact, however, especially in his letters to Princess Elisabeth, Descartes accepts the union of soul and body as given in experience. The two worlds, one of extension and the other of thought, make contact at this one point. The connection of the body with the soul, he would say, is that the former is the machine the latter directs. The direction takes place in the brain, more particularly in the pineal gland and through the medium of the "animal spirits" it controls. This small gland is "the main seat of the soul" and is "suspended between the cavities which contain the spirits". Stimuli from outer objects act on the senses and through the animal spirits on the gland. In some cases, the response to these by "the machine of the body" is independent of the soul; in other cases "passions are excited in the soul". And, finally, the soul may initiate action when,

> solely because it desires something, it causes the little gland to which it is closely united to move in the way requisite to produce the effect which relates to this desire.[12]

Descartes bequeathed to posterity a world cut in two, divided between matter and mind. The exception made in favour of man did not seriously affect the picture. A. N. Whitehead is one of those who have seen in the 'Cartesian dualism' an unfortunate influence. Descartes, he says, created

> a private world of passions, or modes, of independent substance.

Also the independence ascribed to bodily sub-

[11] *Oeuvres*, 1909, XI, p, 120.
[12] *Philosophical Works of Descartes*, trans. Haldane and Ross, 1911, Vol. I, pp. 347-350.

stances carried them away from the realm of values altogether. They degenerated into a mechanism entirely valueless, except as suggestive of an external ingenuity. The heavens had lost the glory of God.[13]

CHAPTER IV   Truth and Error

IN the account given of Descartes' thought in the previous sections, his experiment in doubt was taken as the starting-point. There was however an alternative available in his criterion of truth. His earliest publication bore the title *Rules for the Direction of the Mind,* and in this he tried to show how we can pass "sound and true judgments on all that presents itself to us".[14] The book was never finished: as we have it, it contains twenty-one rules instead of the thirty-six originally contemplated. Elsewhere he reduces the number to four, which we may summarize thus:

1. Accept as true only what is apprehended so clearly and distinctly that you cannot doubt it.

2. Break up each problem into as many parts as it will yield, and tackle these in turn.

3. Observe an order in your inquiry, passing from the simple to the complex, from what is easy to understand to what is more difficult.

4. Make sure of covering the whole ground.[15]

The expression 'clear and distinct' has been used, and this is so important that an explanation is called for. As we have seen, for Descartes the ultimate certainty is self-consciousness. This then yields a criterion of truth. What stamps itself on the mind, as it were, with equal force, what is as immediately and indubitably convincing as self-consciousness, will be true. Or, as he puts it, when an idea is clear and distinct its truth is thereby guaranteed.

Having noted that in this proposition (I think,

[13] *Science and the Modern World,* 1937, p. 242.
[14] Smith: *Op. cit.,* p. 3.
[15] *Ibid.,* pp. 129f.

therefore I am) nothing assures me of its truth save only that I see very clearly that in order to think it is necessary to be, I judged that I could take it as being a general rule, that the things we apprehend very clearly and distinctly are true.[16]

What is meant by 'clear and distinct'? Descartes tells us.

I call that clear which is present and manifest to the mind giving attention to it, just as we are said clearly to see objects when being present to the eye looking on, they stimulate it with sufficient force and it is disposed to regard them; but the distinct is that which is so precise and different from all other objects as to comprehend in itself only what is clear.[17]

Perhaps the best approach to Descartes' view of truth is by comparing it with two others that have had considerable following. The common sense view is that truth consists in agreement between the ideas in our mind and the external things or facts to which they refer. But if—as is assumed—I have access only to the ideas, how can I know whether they correspond to anything or not? Descartes meets this difficulty by an appeal to God, who is altogether veracious. Since he is good, he will not allow me to be deceived by ideas that are clear and distinct and yet have nothing to them. Another view is that truth either consists in, or is evidenced by, the coherence of our ideas. Most of us reject a person's claim to have seen a ghost on this ground; it just does not square with the rest of our knowledge. Descartes' practice would no doubt accept this, but his theory does not. For him, each idea is cut off from the rest; it is not part of a continuum of experience or a body of knowledge, but stands on its own feet. It is therefore true or false in itself and not in relation to other ideas.[18]

---

[16] *Ibid.*, p. 141. The rest of the passage will be given later.

[17] Everyman's Library, p. 182.

[18] Something should be said about the confusion rampant in Descartes' treatment of ideas. The term covers (i) the mental process of referring to an object (ii) the object referred to (iii) the mental image that sometimes, but not always, accompanies (i).

If all this is the case, we are puzzled to know how, if all clear and distinct ideas are true and are guaranteed by God, we ever fall into error. We may now complete the quotation on an earlier page. Such ideas are true—"bearing in mind, however, that there is some difficulty in rightly determining which are those we apprehend distinctly".[19]

In a footnote above, attention was drawn to three senses in which Descartes used the word 'idea'. We have now to take account of a fourth, one for which the word 'judgment' would be much better. Immediate awareness does not admit of the distinction between truth and falsehood; this arises only when we form a judgment on that of which we are aware. When I say 'this pen is black' I may be mistaken. What I see is actually a pencil or gray, and some trick of its position or the light deceives me. The fault lies not in the sense-impression as such but in how I interpret it, and my simplest statements about what I perceive contain some element of interpretation.

The correct question is therefore not how we have false ideas but how we come to pass erroneous judgments. The fault, we are told, lies with the will, though the mind may be an accomplice before the fact. Not all our ideas are actually clear and distinct. Better, we entertain in the mind judgments that are neither self-evident nor clearly established. But instead of suspending any further decision on them till we have more to go on, we may decide, as our freedom allows us to do, to accept such a judgment as true here and now. When the evidence is all in, it turns out that we were wrong. Error is grounded in that freedom by which we are distinguished from the animal. "To err is human." What makes it particularly easy to err is that we are not limited to what we perceive, but can and must make statements about the past. And how defective memory is! Indeed, we sometimes make assertions about the past in entire good faith, and they turn out to have nothing whatever to them.

One more topic calls to be considered before we conclude this section, that of the place and significance of 'innate ideas' for Descartes. General notions such as the propositions of mathematics are not, he would say,

[19] Smith: *Op. cit.*, p. 142.

derived from sense-perception, which gives us blurred information and not clear-cut concepts. We are therefore driven to think that such ideas are part of the original furniture of the human mind. The same applies to the idea of God. These are instances of innate ideas. But exactly what this implies it is hard to say. Where he expresses himself most clearly on the subject, he appears to mean simply that we are so made that we must think along lines that, when we come to understand them, can be elaborated into the system of mathematics or yield a full-fledged concept of God. Innate ideas, we are told, are "contained in the mind, only in *power,* and not in *act*". We are "created with the faculty of thinking and forming them", so that they are innate in all men as generosity and alcoholism are said to be innate in some families: i.e., members of those families are born predisposed thereto.[20] He disclaims any suggestion that we arrive in the world with a stock of ready-made information, though this is what his critics took him to maintain, not altogether without reason.

CHAPTER V   Freedom

LET us now look more closely into this dangerous privilege of freedom that man enjoys. Descartes claims that freedom is absolute and infinite. As Sartre says today, echoing him in this, we have all the freedom there is. The will "in its kind" is "altogether ample and perfect".

> I am conscious of a will so extended as to be subject to no limits. . . .
> Free will alone, that is liberty of choice, do I find to be so great in me that I can entertain no idea of any such power possibly greater, so that it is chiefly my will which enables me to know that I bear a certain image and similitude of God.[21]

He goes on to say that while, of course, "the power of will is indeed incomparably greater in God than in

[20] Everyman's Library, p. 252.
[21] Smith: *Op. cit.,* pp. 235f.

man", because of the knowledge etc. associated with it, yet in itself, *qua* will, "it does not seem to be greater". The language is startling enough at first glance and becomes yet more so on examination. When at the beginning of the medieval scholastic development, Anselm wanted to demonstrate God's existence, he set out from our knowledge of him as "an idea, than which none greater can be conceived". So Descartes now speaks of our freedom!

Since there is this correspondence between freedom in man and in God, we ask how Descartes presents the latter. God is absolute will and could, had he so chosen, have made a world different at all points from the one we inhabit. It is not merely that trees might, at his will, have grown with their roots in the air and their branches in the ground. Twice two makes four simply because God willed that it should be so, and it was within his power to make the result some other figure. This is William of Occam come again. The principles of morals and of mathematics are equally dependent on a divine decision that might have gone otherwise. No doubt, this is most difficult to grasp. But that is due merely to the limits of human understanding. We can see how those things are possible that God willed to be possible, for they are here before us. But how those things he willed to be impossible might have been possible—there's the rub. That there are eternal and necessary truths Descartes does not for a moment question; the point he is concerned to make is that God has willed them to be eternal and necessary. He might equally have made them contingent and transient. He just did not, and it is useless for us to ask why. One difficulty, however, proves insuperable. In correspondence with Father Mesland, Descartes confesses himself baffled by the puzzle: Could God have made creatures so that they were not dependent on him? In other words; Could he have made creatures that were not creatures. If we put it like that, we can say that the question is unanswerable because it does not make sense.

This way of thinking affects Descartes' view of creation. The creation of the world cannot be for him the bringing into being of an order that is acknowledged and respected by God as other than himself and subject to its own laws. This, I take it, is the traditional Chris-

110

tian position, as shown by the fact that when the theologian has finished his chapter on creation he adds to it one on providence. In providence God maintains the world on the lines on which he created it at first. But for Descartes creation and providence fuse, yielding a continuous creative activity on the part of God. Nor is this the case only with the material world. The same is true of each human being. We hang as it were over an abyss of nothingness, supported merely by something for which there is no guarantee, God's decision to create us afresh at this moment as he did at the previous one.

The course of my life can be divided into innumerable parts, none of which is in any way dependent on the others. Accordingly it does not follow that because I was in existence a short time ago I must be in existence now, unless there be some cause which produces me, creates me as it were anew at this very instant, that is to say, conserves me. To all those who consider with attention the nature of time it is indeed evident that a thing in order to be conserved at each of the moments in which it endures has need of the same power and action as would be required to produce and create it anew, if it did not yet exist. That the difference between creation and conservation is a difference solely in our way of thinking is one of the many things which the natural light manifests to us.[22]

The dominant feature of such a world is discontinuity. Everything breaks up into a series of atomic states with no connection between them. Time is not an ever-rolling stream; it is a succession of time-drops. Experience is not growth and a process of learning; it is a string of ideas, each cut off from the rest. The state of the world at one moment does not continue what is was a moment before; it is a fresh creation. How can we live, if we take seriously such an account? Not by a devout trust in the faithfulness of God. For, on this scheme, does the faithfulness of God mean more than that *so far* he has willed to be self-consistent? What he will choose to do in the future we do not know.

I return to the subject of human freedom. We have seen that the pineal gland is the point at which the

[22] *Ibid.*, pp. 227f.

interaction of mind and body, otherwise so impossible, takes place. Thus, sense-objects cause 'passions' in the soul, which in turn seeks to bring the passions under control. What is often described as the conflict between reason and desire becomes for Descartes a struggle to possess and direct the animal spirits.

> There is, therefore, no contest save that which takes place in the small gland which is in the centre of the brain, when it is impelled to one side by the soul, and to another by the animal spirits which, as above said, are entirely corporeal; often the two impacts are contrary to one another; and the stronger holds the other in check.[23]

Something momentous has taken place. The champion of absolute freedom over against the mechanisms of nature has now extended mechanism to the soul. What appears to be decision is but the resultant of the impact of two forces on the same object.

CHAPTER VI   Successors of Descartes

THE modern reader may be critical of Descartes, but he cannot, for all that, escape his influence. He did not originate the mechanical view of the world, but it did receive from him a statement that gave it a lasting hold upon the Western mind. After him, it advanced from one success to another. Even those who deny that mechanism *explains* anything may yet use it as the best available method for the *description* of natural processes. The problem of body and mind is still with us, and it needs no little effort to grasp the possibility that, instead of trying to solve it, we should refuse to accept it in the form in which he expressed it. Above all, whenever we fix on self-consciousness as the one sure point from which we can set out to extend our knowledge, we are consciously or unconsciously his followers.

Descartes left behind him an inheritance into which

[23] *Ibid.*, p. 302.

many entered, both in France and in England. But more important than those who developed his system were those whom it provoked to opposition. Greatest among these is Spinoza, the Netherlands Jew whom Church and Synagogue disowned, who was branded in his own time as an atheist yet came to be celebrated as "the God-intoxicated man", and in our time has received the dubious compliment of inclusion among the forerunners of dialectical materialism. He accepted the dualism of thought and extension only to resolve it in a higher unity. They are not two separate substances, for to understand what 'substance' means is to see that there can be only one. They are the two attributes under which we apprehend that one infinite substance to which, borrowing from his Jewish monotheistic tradition, he gave the name of God. God does not create or cause; all things follow necessarily from his nature, as the conclusion of an argument from its premises. The eternal truths that Descartes grounded in the will of God have therefore a surer foundation in his being. But, by the same token, there is no room in Spinoza's system for what we normally mean by freedom. We too follow necessarily from the one substance. Freedom as a moral achievement is extolled, however, though perhaps by a defect in logic. It is the condition of release from passion to which the wise man attains when he sees all things from the perspective of eternity, as they flow from the being of God. Spinoza created one of those magnificent structures in which only the mean-minded will strut about to detect flaws: it is to be appreciated and admired as a whole, though admiration may not prevent our rejecting it in the end.

John Locke, on the other hand, launched an attack on innate ideas and replaced them by the conception of the mind as a blank sheet of paper on which objects in the external world or our own psychological processes leave an impression. This is no more satisfactory than the account of knowledge it was meant to displace, but its consequences were far-reaching. Granted that the mind of the child is empty and waiting to be filled from without, what a vista opens out before the educationist! The human material is plastic in his hands. Man is no longer thought of as burdened with original sin; soon he will need only direction—and time—to reach perfection. Archimedes said that, given a point to stand on, he would move the world. The eighteenth century came into possession of two such points; they were Locke's theory of knowledge and Newton's physics.

For further reading:

Translations by J. Veitch, E. S. Haldane and G. R. T. Ross, Norman Kemp Smith, and E. Anscombe and P. T. Geach.

S. V. Keeling: *Descartes.*

N. K. Smith: *New Studies in Descartes.*

PART SEVEN

KANT

CHAPTER I   The Problem of Knowledge

THE last chapter closed with Spinoza and Locke. These
two men may be taken as representative of two tendencies that the seventeenth century handed on to the
eighteenth. The tendencies in question, rationalism and
empiricism, the appeal to first principles and the appeal
to experience, were of course much older. The rationalists
were allured by mathematics with its ability to deduce
a rich variety of propositions and theorems from a few
initial axioms, and they supposed that this procedure
could be applied to all worth-while knowledge. The
fundamental axiom for their enterprise was the Principle of Sufficient Reason, that a thing cannot be both
A and not-A. A pencil may be sharp today and blunt
tomorrow; but if I once say it is sharp and then go on,
in the same context, to say it is not sharp and to draw
conclusions from that, I shall fall into error. This
sounds commonplace enough, but it means that strict
self-consistency is the path to truth. Leibniz supplemented this axiom by a second, the Principle of Sufficient Reason, that

> in virtue of which we hold that there can be no fact
> real or existing, no statement true, unless there be a
> sufficient reason why it should be so and not other-
> wise, although these reasons usually cannot be known
> by us.[1]

Empiricists like Locke were doubtful about this recourse to first principles and preferred what is observed,
the hard fact to which we must do justice if we are not

---

[1] *The Monadology* etc., trans. R. Latta, 1925, p. 235.

to build castles in the air. He was followed by Berkeley, who bade us note that this hard fact is what the common man takes it to be, that which he actually perceives, and not at all what the philosophers took it to be, some mysterious inaccessible matter lying behind this. Hume pushed still further the inquiry as to what is actually there and came to an even more disturbing conclusion. Descartes began with 'I doubt', but Hume could find no 'I' at all. He was himself—and he made bold to affirm the same of the rest of mankind—only

> a bundle or collection of different perceptions, which succeed each other with an inconceivable rapidity, and are in a perpetual flux and movement.[2]

If the foundations were thus rudely removed, how much of the building would remain? Nothing would be left of the most imposing and most frequented wing, that over which stood the inscription: God, Freedom, Immortality. Hume announced the bankruptcy of metaphysics. The volumes of natural theology on the philosopher's shelves would be more appropriately accommodated in his fireplace! When Kant was a student first and afterwards a teacher at Königsberg, the rationalism of which I have spoken was dominant in Germany and he himself belonged to that school. Its leading representative was Christian Wolff, who taught in Halle and Marburg (1697-1754). Kant tells us that it was the reading of Hume that woke him from his "dogmatic slumber". But he was not prepared to dismiss the ultimate questions outright. He had no intention of feeding his fire as Hume recommended. *Some* way there must be to God, freedom, and immortality, though it could not be that of mere reasoning. Metaphysics refused to succumb to the harsh treatment Hume gave it, as it declines to vanish today when the logical positivist waves his wand.

Now, there was at the time one realm in which certain results had been achieved, in which, as it seemed to Kant, truth had been attained once and for all. That was Newtonian physics. We today have learned from

[2] *A Treatise of Human Nature*, ed. L. A. Selby-Bigge, 1896, p. 252.

Einstein to think of the classical physics not as universal in application, but as valid for a special case that is also the most familiar one, the world of man-sized objects. Within the atom it breaks down. Such doubts were as yet far away. The genius of Newton had carried to its completion the work of his predecessors in several fields. The mechanical principles which had been applied to the terrestrial realm now took over the celestial as well. It was a triumph of applied mathematics, which in one magnificent generalization, the law of gravitation, covered the fall of an apple, the movements of the heavenly bodies, and all that lay between. The most striking achievement of the new physics was its ability to predict, so that today scientists can organize years ahead to observe an eclipse on a certain date. There is something uncanny about this procedure. You can outrun experience and make statements about what has yet to be observed and be sure that you will prove correct. What enables you to do this is, first, that at some point you set out from observed data and propose finally to return to observable data, and, second, that you operate in accordance with the rules of mathematics. The procedure is neither that of the rationalist nor that of the empiricist, yet does it not seem also to be a bit of both?

The time seemed to Kant ripe for a new kind of inquiry. Let us give up the attempt to deduce everything from certain innate ideas, and also the restriction of the mind to what streams in through the senses. Why not inquire just what the powers of the mind are, what we can hope to know and where we must be content to be ignorant? He was not the first to offer such a suggestion: Locke had preceded him. But what Locke provided scarcely filled the bill. It was an account of how 'ideas' got into our minds and were sorted out there. Kant wanted to know, not how we got our knowledge, but how reliable it is. He called his philosophy therefore the critical philosophy and the first great work in which he undertook this inquiry *The Critique of Pure Reason*. His solution of the problem might be put in Aristotelian terms. The empiricists are right, inasmuch as the *matter* of knowledge is furnished by the senses, the rationalists also right, inasmuch as its *form* is supplied by the understanding. The next three sections will attempt to elucidate this.

CHAPTER II   Space and Time

PERHAPS an illustration, however inadequate, may serve to explain what Kant means by this suggestion. Let us suppose that we are hearing evidence from a number of persons as to what happened on a certain occasion. After several have spoken, someone comes forward whose evidence is so clear and convincing that no more is needed. He knows what has happened, we say. But what is involved in saying that he 'knows'? For one thing, he is able to locate events in space and time, to say where they happened and in what order, as opposed to the man who is hazy on such points. Then he is able to link up events so as to show their interconnection and to present a coherent account, as opposed to the man who merely strings one item after another. Finally, he has an idea of what is wanted, of the purpose his story is to serve, and can therefore cut out what is not essential, as opposed to the man who introduces irrelevant material. What gives his evidence its superiority to that of others, assuming, to be sure, that all were equally near to what happened? It is his personal qualities, he has the kind of mind that can handle what he observed and make a story out of it.

We pass now from one particular item of knowledge to a whole body of knowledge, the physical science of Kant's day. Here the same factors are at work and seem to operate at three distinct levels. First, all events with which the physicist deals fall within space and time; if they did not, they would lie outside his province. Second, they are linked together by various relations, pre-eminently that of cause and effect. We should not call a man a physicist who merely told us that there was *some* relation between *a* and *b*; if he can tell us that *a* is the cause of *b* and even give us a mathematical formula to cover this, we consider his claim seriously. Third, there is also an ideal of complete knowledge, of a system in which everything falls into place, that inspires the scientist. Thus Newton was not content to call a halt at the point he had reached; he expressed the hope "that we could derive the rest of the phenomena of nature by the same kind of reasoning from mechanical principles".[3] The scientist never completes his knowledge, but he never abandons the effort to do so. This third point brings out what might otherwise have been overlooked; the scientist himself makes a major contribution to what comes about. He sees connections where others see none, for example. Science is as much interpretation as observation, perhaps more so.

We have still to reach what Kant is after. Our scientific knowledge is a systematization of common sense knowledge. Adults who have lost the sense of continuity in time and contiguity in space, who cannot see the connection between events, have to be put in someone's charge. They cannot live and work in the actual world. Kant suggests that the factors we have singled out apply to all knowledge of the physical world. Such knowledge is of objects in space and time as these are interconnected within a unifying system, and under the guidance of directives that point whither we are to travel, though we shall not expect to arrive. He calls these factors respectively *the forms of intuition, the categories of the understanding,* and *the ideas of reason.* Whence do they come? From the human mind, from a style of thinking common to us all and in virtue of which we are human and not animal. All knowledge is by interpretation and we prescribe the terms in which the interpretation is to be carried out.

Kant called this new approach the 'Copernican revolution' in philosophy. He proposed that, instead of assuming that our understanding must conform to objects, we should try the hypothesis that "objects must conform to our knowledge."[4] We are the makers of nature! A startling suggestion indeed, till we reflect that what Kant means by nature is a system of objects manifesting an order on which predictions can be based. Since we make it not arbitrarily but by the way in which our minds function, we know in advance that whatever turns up within it will comply with the conditions laid down by our mind. In this way we possess a knowledge of what will be experienced without having

[3] Quoted in H. G. Alexander: *The Leibniz-Clarke Correspondence,* 1956, pp. 144f.
[4] *Critique of Pure Reason,* trans. Norman Kemp Smith, 1933, p. 22.

had recourse to experience to find out. As Kant puts it synthetic *a priori* propositions are possible: they are synthetic as giving new knowledge, *a priori* as not derived from sense-experience. A modern scientist who is in sympathy with Kant uses the image of a net. An ichthyologist drops a net of certain dimensions in the sea and on the basis of his catch makes statements about all sea-creatures. The physical scientist, he goes on, works in similar fashion. His selection is subjective, dependent on our sensory and intellectual equipment.

It is to such objectively-selected knowledge, and to the universe which it is formulated to describe, that the generalizations of physics—the so-called laws of nature—apply.[5]

Kant would say that we know appearances only and not things-in-themselves.

As beings with sense-organs, we apprehend all that occurs to us and that we regard as other than ourselves (the external world) as ordered in space and time. This is to the left of that, *a* was before *b*. What belongs to inner experience, the flow of mental process, is in time but not in space. And space and time, according to Kant, are supplied by ourselves as having senses.[6] They are forms of intuition, forms under which we apprehend particular phenomena, whether in the external world or in ourselves. This presupposes, however, that something is given us to apprehend. Whence does this come? From the senses as these are affected by a mysterious *x or x's* that make impact thereon, things-in-themselves. *That* there are such we can be sure; *what* they are must remain unknown to us. They are a text to which we have access only in translation.

[5] A. Eddington: *The Philosophy of Physical Science,* 1939, p. 17.
[6] Animals will therefore operate with space and time, but God will not.

The Understanding

LET us consider what is involved in so simple a procedure as perceiving an orange. I can report on its colour, shape, size and so on; I bite it, and can make yet another statement about it. I leave it lying for a few minutes, I return to it and perceive it again. There is much more here than merely noting a succession of data offered by the senses and related to each other in space and time. I apprehend the orange as a unity, a synthesis of these different data. I take it for granted that something permanent is involved; there is an object—the orange—that persists in spite of undergoing change. But now what is meant by 'I'? There again I seem to be assuming persistence through change, a centre of unity. For do I not correlate what I perceive as an orange now with what I perceived five minutes ago? It is not possible to speak of what happens in such a case except on the assumption that the 'I' is one in the two experiences. Kant would say therefore that the perception of an object is possible only in virtue of a unifying activity on the part of the mind.

This activity takes place at the level of understanding and by the application of categories and principles to what is perceived. Understanding is common to us all as possessed of intelligence, so that it can be termed 'consciousness in general'. The activity by which this synthesizes the data supplied by the senses and makes objects out of them Kant calls 'the transcendental unity of apperception'. That is transcendental which does not fall within our experience as part of it, but it presupposed in it, constitutes it, makes it possible for us to have experience at all. The understanding, we are told, "prescribes laws to nature, and even makes nature possible".[7] For nature, as Kant uses the term, is a system of interrelated objects, and such a system is possible only because there is an understanding to weave into objects the data given by the senses and to connect them according to laws. To understand Kant here, we

[7] *Critique of Pure Reason*, p. 170.

must give up the notion that we first know things and then interpret them. We only know as we interpret. Now we can see how knowledge that runs ahead of experience is possible. Just as, before I pick up a penny, I know that it will have a date on it though not what the date will be, so I know in advance that any object I meet with will be in space and time, connected with other objects, caused, and so on. That is what being an object means. Now, too, we can see the significance of the forms of intuition, especially space. Since all objects fall within space, it follows that mathematical principles and calculations are applicable to them.

Just as nature is measurable in virtue of the forms of intuition, so it has the character of law in virtue of the categories of understanding. We need not consider how Kant reaches these categories, especially as he does so in a way scarcely anyone since has found convincing. The three most important are substance, cause, and community, and the principles in accordance with which they are applied run thus:

> In all change of appearance substance is permanent; its quantum in nature is neither increased nor diminished.
> All alterations take place in conformity with the law of the connexion of cause and effect.
> All substances, in so far as they can be perceived to coexist in space, are in thoroughgoing reciprocity.[8]

Without these guiding lines, not merely would no physics be possible; there would be no experience. We should be reduced to what William James called "a blooming, buzzing confusion". These principles are supplied by the mind, that is, by what is common to all our minds, so that what it constructs is objective as far as we individually are concerned.

The crucial case is the category of cause. Kant was greatly impressed by Hume's treatment of this. The latter denied that an inspection of our experience would yield any necessary connection between *a* and *b* that would justify our saying that *a* was the cause of *b*. What in fact happened was that *b* so often followed *a* for our observation that we got into the habit, when one

[8] *Ibid.*, pp. 212, 218, 233.

occurred, of looking for the other. Kant agreed that experience does not yield a necessary cause-effect connection. Since, in his view, necessity is inherent in the concept, it must be supplied by the understanding. That nature is a system of causal laws on which predictions can be based is not something we merely observe; it is something we bring about, and only thereafter can it be observed. His argument against Hume is that we must distinguish between the case in which *b* follows *a* because we have turned our attention to them in that order and might have done otherwise (as when my eye travels from the top of a house to the bottom) and the case in which the order is fixed and independent of us (as when, in building a house, I must begin at the bottom). The language of cause and effect is used only in the second case, where the connection is necessary; as Hume saw, necessity cannot be perceived, so it must come from the understanding. Not, of course, your understanding or mine, but understanding as functioning in all of us.[9]

It must not be thought that Kant is describing a process that runs through successive stages. We do not first passively receive sensations from outside, then arrange these in space and time, and finally impose the categories on them. The knowing process is a unity: when we come to analyze it, we can distinguish these three aspects within it, but they have no separate existence.

CHAPTER IV   The Ideas of Reason

THE forms of intuition, the categories of the understanding—what next? We come next to the ideas of reason. These are three in number, the soul, the world, and God. We shall get to know them best by watching them at work. The psychologist studies the different types of mental functioning, making statements about instinct, memory, sensation, etc. He works all the while on the assumption that he is concerned with various aspects

[9] Space does not permit of an attempt to deal with what Kant says of the imagination and its schemata as mediating between the categories and the percepts to which they are applied.

of something he envisages as a unity. This something nowadays he will call mind or consciousness. In Kant's time he would probably have used the word 'soul'. He is driven by the desire to get ever fuller knowledge of this and nothing can satisfy him short of exhaustive knowledge. Yet he must never imagine that he has gained this exhaustive knowledge and is in a position to talk about the soul as though it were one more object like a sensation or a visual image. When he forms sentences like 'The soul is immortal' he is speaking no longer as a psychologist but as a metaphysician, and this he has no right to do. It is the same with physics. The scientist operates *as if* there were a world of which he is obtaining ever more complete knowledge. But his knowledge is always partial, and therefore statements about the world as though it were an object one could view from outside, like the atom, are not scientific propositions but metaphysical ventures.

What this means is that the ideas of reason are regulative and not constitutive. They do not give us information about objects, they direct us in our investigation of objects. The scientist must always try to fit together the results at which he arrives, regarding them as parts of a body of knowledge that, when completed, will form a coherent system; yet he must never suppose that he is in possession of such a system. It is an ideal that lures him on yet always evades him. Kant is opposing the rationalism that was rife in his early days, and that allowed philosophers to set out from a concept of the soul or the world and deduce something they sought to pass off as knowledge. He will have none of this. Knowledge is of appearances and not of things-in-themselves, about what we observe and not about what lies behind this. Statements about what happens in space and time according to the laws that emanate from the understanding—these constitute knowledge. What goes beyond this does not do so, though it may stimulate and guide our quest for knowledge.

Kant defines the ideas of reason as

the absolute unity of the thinking subject . . . the absolute unity of the series of conditions of appearance . . . the absolute unity of the condition of all objects of thought in general.[10]

[10] *Ibid.*, p. 323.

The third idea is that of God. And now the question is raised: can God's existence be proved? We have seen how, from the Greeks onward, the Western mind made an effort to reach God by the way of reasoning. This effort might be in opposition to the prevalent religion, as in Aristotle, or in alliance with it, as in Aquinas and, to a less extent, Descartes. Only a minority of thinkers had been sceptical of such an enterprise. What Kant does is to consider the various arguments for God's existence that have been put forward and to find them one and all invalid. He dismisses them on two grounds. In the first place, he singles out the weak points in each argument. In the second, he directs against them the general consideration that demonstration is valid only for objects in space and time and subject to the principles with which the understanding operates. God is by definition not such an object. Therefore demonstration is not possible in his case. But, for the same reason, there is no argument that disproves him. To be God is to transcend the realm to which demonstration applies.

Yet Kant is aware that quite eminent philosophers have thought they were talking sense when they made statements about the soul—Plato certainly did—and the world, and even when they tried to demonstrate God's existence. Nor does he suppose that his negative treatment of these three subjects will persuade men henceforth to abandon them. Metaphysics is certainly not science, but it corresponds to a permanent disposition of the human mind. When we think it is a science we are victims of an illusion Kant is sure he can explain. Because the ideas of reason are indispensable to the *pursuit* of knowledge, we fall into the error of supposing that they correspond to objects just like those of which we can *have* knowledge. In the terms he employs, we take as constitutive what is regulative. Because they are indispensable guides to information about objects, we slip into regarding them as objects about which we have information. That they never are. Not that they are just useful fictions, working hypotheses that may in fact have nothing to them. They are pointers to what transcends the realm in which science operates, the realm of things-in-themselves. How we have access to this realm the next section will show.

So far we have been concerned with what Kant calls the theoretical reason, using the term now in a broad sense as covering perception and understanding also. It is the kind of reason that gives us, in its crude form, common sense knowledge of the world we live in, and, in its refined form, Newtonian physics. What Kant seeks to establish is that this reason gives certainty within its limits. It gives certainty because it is itself the source of nature's regularities. It has limits because, this being the case, it is confined to its own product. We have indubitable knowledge—of appearances. Not, be it reiterated, appearances to you and me merely, but appearances to human beings as such. What depends on 'consciousness-in-general' is objective enough as far as we are concerned. Science has been transformed since Kant, but his conclusion stands. It can give us so much only because it is so limited in its range. There is therefore still value in the *Critique of Pure Reason* as "at the same time a hymn to the creative powers of reason and an elegy on its limitations".[11]

CHAPTER V   Ethics

THEORETICAL reason resembles a building in three floors. We have now reached the top floor and look out over a stretch of country wider and richer than that on which the building stands. That country is the home of practical reason, reason, that is, as it is at work in moral judgments and moral conduct. For Kant it is of the very essence of morality that it be disinterested. A good act done to please somebody or to gain an advantage or to secure a reward from God would cease thereby to be good; it would fall to the level of mere expediency. An action should be done because the doer sees for himself that it is right, that it is his duty. Or one may say that the moral imperative is categorical and not hypothetical. That is to say, it does not run: 'If you want society to prosper or your own property to be secure, then do not steal', but simply: 'Thou shalt not steal!' It comes to us as a law requiring unconditional obedience. We do not make it but find it; yet as rational beings we obey it because we impose it upon ourselves.

[11] Gottfried Martin: *Kant's Metaphysics and Theory of Science,* trans. P. G. Lucas, 1955, p. 126.

The command of an external authority, be it God himself, is binding on us only as it wins the recognition of our conscience.

Can we further define this moral law? Since it is absolute and universal and has nothing to do with prudential considerations though everything to do with the fact that we are rational, we may define it (a) from the very notion of a universal law and (b) from the very notion of a rational being. We then have two formulations; (a) *Act only on that maxim* (or principle) *that you can at the same time will to be a universal law;* (b) *Treat everyone as an end in himself and never merely as means to an end.* The second hardly calls for comment. In the first, the operative word is 'will'. When a man commits suicide or steals, Kant would say that he cannot seriously *will* that everybody should do the same. What he wills is in fact that other people should live to provide for those he leaves behind, or that they shall be honest enough for him to rely on them when he wants to dispose of what he has stolen. The evildoer sets up as an exception. He wants to have both the advantages that come from his breaking the moral law and those that depend on others respecting it. The detailed application of Kant's formula no doubt raises difficulties, but the principle itself embodies an insight of permanent value. Notoriously, the enemy of freedom and constitutional procedure has a vested interest in the respect that others pay to them.

Granted that morality is as Kant describes it, there are certain consequences that appear to be involved in it. The first is *freedom.* I cannot be under an obligation to do what is not in my power. It cannot be my duty to add ten feet to my stature or to visit the moon. But I am under an obligation to obey the moral law. To do so must therefore be within my power. "I ought, therefore I can." [12] In the *Critique of Pure Reason* Kant had argued that freedom is *possible* in spite of the fact that the inner life as something observed and studied is as much subject to law as is the external world. In both cases, we know only appearances. The self as a thing-in-itself escapes our observation and description.

[12] It should be added that Kant was not blind to the darker aspects of human life. See the section "on the radical evil in human nature" in *Theory of Ethics,* trans. T. K. Abbott.

In his ethical philosophy Kant shows that freedom is *actual*, with moral experience as evidence for it. As *phenomenon* (appearance) man is subject to causal laws; as *noumenon* (thing-in-itself) he is free. He is a member of two worlds at once. As a denizen of the lower world, he is one among many objects; as a citizen of the higher world, he is rational and sovereign, giving laws to himself. Morality arises from the fact that he is neither wholly one nor the other, but a bit of both. He is therefore under the obligation to act according to the requirements of reason in the world of sense and nature. Perhaps we do not pervert Kant's argument if we give it a modern turn. When my choice has been made and lapses into the general stock of nature, I can see it as something that followed on what went before. Yet to acquiesce in that account is to surrender my dignity as a person. I must avow responsibility for what happened. It was my deed.

There are two further inferences from moral experience. The moral law demands perfection; since this is so, it must be within our power. Clearly, perfection is beyond us as we are now, subject to the limitations of life in this world. We must therefore suppose that beyond this world we shall have the opportunity of advancing ever nearer to the goal. That is we must believe in *immortality*. Then, we have not only a duty to do what is right but also a duty to promote the happiness of others. We desire a state of things in which goodness is accompanied by the happiness it deserves. We could not be content to see good for ever in the dungeon and evil for ever on the throne. But happiness belongs to the realm of what *is* and duty to that of what *ought to be*, and only the latter is within the range of our freedom. We must therefore postulate, believe that there is *God* who can bring the two realms together and effect the union of goodness and happiness. This again is a rational faith, something that is required if the moral life is to make sense.

As we look back on Kant's philosophy from the point now reached, two features call for special attention. (1) The old method of inferring God from nature is abandoned. Nature does not give us God, nor does it refuse him. He is not to be spoken of in its language, but in that of conscience, duty, and the moral law. (2) Kant reverses the traditional relation between morality and religion. The former does not depend on the latter, as had been generally assumed hitherto. Moral standards do not require religious belief to justify them; rather we can find God only as we accept moral standards as in themselves authoritative. The question 'Why be good?' would have seemed to Kant an utterly immoral one.

CHAPTER VI   Beauty and Purpose

IN what precedes Kant has given us two worlds, one of things-in-themselves and the other of appearances, one of freedom and the other of nature. The world we actually live in, however, combines the two aspects. He is therefore conscious of the need to adjust these two standpoints, and the *Critique of Judgment* was written for this purpose. We have seen that the principles with which understanding operates gives us nature as a system of law, of law, that is, in such general terms as that every effect has a cause, the changing implies something that is permanent amid change, and so on. But these laws of high generality are not directly applied to observed data in science. Between the two intervene a number of laws that are derived from observation and experiment and that state what cause *a* is operative in a particular case *b*. Sense does not give such a law of itself, nor does understanding. Kant therefore calls into play a third faculty, the Judgment, to perform this office. Now we do not regard these empirical generalizations of science as a mere collection of unrelated propositions; we try to link them together and make a system out of them. And nature lends itself to this procedure. But why? It is *as if* nature were intended to be known by us; there is a mysterious accord between it and our minds. But are we justified in using such words as 'intention' and 'purpose' of nature?

Before we answer this question, however, we must glance in passing at another. Kant has dealt so far with science, morality, and even religion. What of art? He suggests that the concept of purpose may be illuminating in this connection. We judge a thing to be beautiful, whether in nature or in art, when it is 'purposive without purpose', a design that we appreciate for its own sake and not for any purpose it serves. I watch the sunlight on a waterfall and the sight fills me with wonder and delight. I say that it is perfect, everything is just as it should be, that to contemplate it is an elevating experience, and so on. If you now suggest that the site is ideal for a factory, and that it is a shame to see so much power running to waste, my feeling of pleasure vanishes at once. I enjoy the scene, Kant would say, as one that brings into play all my powers, sense, understanding, and reason, in harmonious fashion—but not *for* something. Aesthetic pleasure is entirely disinterested.

We return to the question raised above. May the language of purpose be used of nature? Kant would say that there is one place where it not only may but must be used, and that in the name of science. For physics is not the only science, as indeed we might have concluded from reading the first *Critique*. Biology has also to be considered. And biology resists reduction to mechanics.

> Absolutely no human reason (in fact no finite reason like ours in quality, however much it may surpass it in degree) can hope to understand the production of even a blade of grass by mere mechanical causes.[13]

The organism, even in its most rudimentary forms, must be appreciated as a whole that is more than the sum of its parts. The parts interact, they maintain the whole, and the whole in its turn maintains them. It is as if it possessed a certain formative power that endows with life material that would otherwise lie entirely within the domain of chemistry and physics. The organism demands categories such as function, end, and purpose if justice is to be done to it. Here is a sure foothold for a teleological approach as opposed to the mechanical one.

But the only purpose we can ascribe to an organism is an immanent one, and one moreover that works at the level of instinct rather than intelligence. We describe it *as if* there were a purpose in it; we do not say that in fact there *is* one. But it has often been asserted that

[13] *Kritik of Judgment,* trans. J. H. Bernard, 1892, p. 326.

there is a purpose behind nature as a whole, God's purpose. Where does Kant stand on this point? He will say that the teleological approach to nature is a useful guide to inquiry, but not more than that. The scientist will approach his special field with the assumption that there is order in it, and the kind of order the human mind can appreciate because it works in that way itself. For example, he often takes it for granted that, of two alternative explanations, the simpler will be more likely to be the right one. But, when we come to think of it, why should nature share our passion for saving labour? All this will help him to carry further his explanation in terms of cause and effect, it will never induce him to abandon such explanations. If we want to affirm a purpose in nature, we must transcend science and take account of man as a moral being. If we think of the world as "a vale of soul-making", the mechanisms of nature can be viewed as serving an end beyond themselves. But we are back again at a rational faith; we have not established anything in the scientific sense.

What then is the final relation between mechanism and teleology? In the first place, they represent two alternative approaches, and we take up one and lay down the other as may be useful for our purpose. Normally, the first method is the fruitful one for physics and the second for biology. Next, since ends can only be realized as means thereto are adopted, it may sometimes be the case that purpose at a higher level uses mechanism at a lower, so that both are present. Thirdly, there is an ultimate perspective from which nature is the sphere in which man is to exercise his responsibility. To speak thus is to give meaning to the word 'creation'. But this is not a demonstration of God, not even a new road to him. There is only one road, the path of duty.

For further reading:

Translations of the *Critique of Pure Reason* by Norman Kemp Smith, of the *Critique of Practical Reason* by T. K. Abbott, and of the *Critique of Judgment* by J. H. Bernard and J. C. Meredith.
Commentaries on the *Critique of Pure Reason* by Norman Kemp Smith and A. C. Ewing, on the *Critique of Judgment* by H. W. Cassirer.
S. Körner: *Kant.*
H. J. Paton; *The Categorical Imperative.*

PART EIGHT

ROUSSEAU

CHAPTER I   Eighteenth Century France

WHEN Jean-Jacques Rousseau came to Paris in 1742 to seek his fortune there, that city was still the cultural centre of Europe, and France, in spite of the extravagances and campaigns of Louis XIV, was still foremost among the European states. To be sure, Louis' successor had frittered away much of his inheritance, because he was unwilling to support capable ministers whose policy was as salutary as it was unpalatable and unable to compensate by success abroad for failure at home. Criticism of the existing system was widespread, and in the *Parlement* of Paris discontent was freely expressed. In the salons of polite society what would now be called 'dangerous thoughts' were freely canvassed, and were all the more enjoyed because there was little intention of acting on them. There were those who, like Montesquieu, cast longing eyes across the Channel and praised the British constitution, though they did not always understand it. Only a century before, Britain had gone through the Whig Revolution, and the flight of James II and the accession of William and Mary had given substance to the notion of popular sovereignty.

The politics and economics of the century are the concern of the historian; ours is rather with the ideas that were current then in France and which Rousseau in part accepted and in part contested. Much of course was not new. Theologians during the wars of religion had asserted the rights of the people and given a sanction to regicide; even classical literature was not without pointers in that direction, as the orators of the Revolution were to argue. One shift in the whole climate of thought came when the Abbé de Saint-Pierre (1658-1743) suggested that the human race was not old and burdened with experience, as had hitherto been supposed, but was in fact only in its infancy, with immense possibilities before it. Man was at the stage at which virtually anything could be made out of him by education, especially if, as Locke had argued, his mind is but a blank sheet on which the environment writes its script of impressions or ideas. The belief in progress and in the perfectibility of mankind had arrived, and its hold over men's minds became so secure that two world wars were needed to shake it.

The intellectual pattern of the age, at least as far as France was concerned, was largely set by a class of people known as the *philosophes*. They were men of letters who employed wit, ridicule, and satire to discredit the political and religious institutions of the time. They saw in them the root of all evil. Men had been too long the dupes of kings and priests, the latter reinforcing the authority of the former by an appeal to unseen powers and their will. Let their claims be examined in the cold, clear light of reason and it would be seen how baseless they were; man would be liberated from all such tyranny and—so some at least imagined —he would demonstrate his natural virtue. The sceptical but cautious Pierre Bayle (1647-1706) was their forerunner, and their great work, the *Encyclopædia*, was modelled on his *Dictionary*. Diderot was one of the best-known members of the group and Rousseau was for a time closely associated with him. Their influence was almost entirely negative; many of them were atheists and some materialists. They had no policy of political and social reform. When Rousseau broke with them it was principally over their irreligion.

The most familiar name of the period is probably that of Voltaire, and it is of interest to the English reader that one of his most influential works was the slim volume of *Letters* (1733) in which he related his experience in England. He did this in such a way as to expose the shortcomings of his own country. He was particularly struck by the toleration of so many different forms of religion and the fact that this policy of 'live and let live' contributed to the prosperity of the nation. The virtues of the Quaker were rewarded by wealth. Of Voltaire himself we may say without being unfair that he had talent but not genius, knowledge but not wisdom.

He expresses the views and arguments of the average educated man in the most felicitous language, with the most marvellous lucidity, and with the most brilliant wit. . . . His influence was so great because he enunciated ideas which were held half unconsciously or timidly by his readers.[1]

Yet our debt to him is not inconsiderable. We recall that he withered with his scorn such practices as torture and urged humanity in the treatment of criminals. Nor was he an atheist, like so many of the *philosophes*. His famous saying that if there were no God it would be necessary to invent him, was probably quite sincere. He was rather a critic than a constructive reformer. He had little that was positive to offer, and had he lived till the Revolution, he would have been horrified by its excesses and contemptuous of its 'liberty, equality and fraternity'. He had always said that the rabble is vile and must be kept under control.

Rousseau came to Paris and made his name there. But his birthplace was the republic of Geneva, which was not then, be it remembered, within the Swiss Confederation. He forfeited citizenship when he renounced Protestantism, but it was a proud moment for him when he recovered it on withdrawing his profession of Catholicism—an empty one from the first. Protestant Geneva was largely the work of Calvin and his spirit lingered in it, even though the harsher elements of his teaching had been repudiated. It was at that period an aristocratic republic with the franchise limited to a fraction of the population and power largely concentrated in a few families. There were those in the city who were democratically minded and advocated a return to the general body of citizens of the rights that, it was alleged, the patricians had filched from them. Popular sovereignty was therefore in the air in republican Geneva as in monarchical France.

[1] P. F. Willert in *Cambridge Modern History*, 1934, VIII, pp. 10f.

CHAPTER II   Rousseau the Man

THE best introduction to Rousseau the man is the one he has himself provided in the opening sentences of the Confessions.

> I have resolved on an enterprise which has no precedent, and which, once complete, will have no imitator. My purpose is to display to my kind a portrait in every way true to nature, and the man I shall portray will be myself.
>
> Simply myself. I know my own heart and understand my fellow man. But I am made unlike anyone I have ever met: I will even venture to say that I am like no one in the whole world. I may be no better, but at least I am different. Whether Nature did well or ill in breaking the mould in which she formed me, is a question which can only be resolved after the reading of my book.
>
> Let the last trump sound when it will, I shall come forward with this work in my hand, to present myself before my Sovereign Judge, and proclaim aloud: 'Here is what I have done, and if by chance I have used some immaterial embellishment it has been only to fill a void due to defect of memory. I may have taken for fact what was no more than probability, but I have never put down as true what I knew to be false. I have displayed myself as I was, as vile and despicable when my behaviour was such, as good, generous, and noble when I was so. I have bared my secret soul as Thou thyself hast seen it, Eternal Being! So let the numberless legions of my fellow men gather round, me, and hear my confessions. Let them groan at my depravities, and blush for my misdeeds. But let each one of them reveal his heart at the foot of Thy throne, and may any man who dares, say 'I was a better man than he'.[2]

[2] Trans. J. M. Cohen, Penguin Classics, 1953.

The principal traits in Rousseau's character are clear at once. He is the egotist who acknowledges himself no better than his fellows, and precisely by making this avowal puts himself above them all in his own eyes. He is the self-made man who avenges himself alike on those who hindered his rise to fame and those who assisted it by relating frankly the part they played in his life. He is the sincere man who imagines that everything will be forgiven if only it is admitted, and whose effort to be sincere is so self-conscious that he strikes a pose and looks round for the admiration of his fellows. And in it all he actually imagines that he sees himself as God sees him! After this, we are not surprised as we go on to read his life-story and fill in the rest of the portrait from it—the lack of any systematic education, the early enthusiasm for the classics, the successive women who attracted or fettered him, the vacillation in religion, the obsession with illness, and the delusions of persecution that grew stronger with the passage of time.

Yet we may not dismiss this man as one more neurotic who has somehow passed himself off as a genius. His influence has proved so great that we must allow that he spoke to some deep need of his time. He has a sure place among those who effected the transition from the Age of Reason to the Romantic Movement. We can single out three important elements in his contribution at this point.

(a) As the passage above cited shows, he laid emphasis on *the unique worth of the individual*. Nature seems to have got into the habit of breaking the mould since Rousseau caught her in the act. In the novel *La Nouvelle Héloïse* he returns to this theme again and again. Lord Edward Boston says of the two lovers, Julie and Saint-Preux: "Your two souls are so extraordinary that you are not to be judged by the common rules". Saint-Preux speaks of "the divine model that he carried within" himself and that "served at once as an object for his desires and as a rule for his actions". We are not surprised to hear of Julie that, as no one had ever lived like her, so she died as no one else ever died.[3] In education, as we shall see, his aim was, not

[3] *Op. cit.,* Partie I, Lettre lv; II, xvii; VI, xi.

to fit the individual into a given social pattern, but to enable him to develop his innate possibilities, to be a man rather than a magistrate, a soldier, or a priest.

(*b*) He represents *the liberation and expression of the emotional life*. Those elements of which the Age of Reason was ashamed come into their own with him. His *Confessions* are a riot of emotion, and *La Nouvelle Héloïse* is a glorification of the tender, introspective soul whose very sins are to be counted redeemed by their aesthetic and emotional quality. Julie gives herself to her lover who is also her tutor and later, under pressure from her father but with her lover's reluctant consent, marries another—and lives happily with him. Her husband is an amateur psychologist and opens his house to Saint-Preux on the latter's return from abroad years later. Julie underwent such a spiritual transformation at her wedding that she is able to meet her lover and even be alone with him by Lake Leman and yet remain unshaken. One character in the novel is frigid, Baron de Wolmar, Julie's husband. But a moment comes when even he is moved.

O feeling, feeling, sweet life of the soul! what heart is so iron as never to have been touched by you? what mortal so unfortunate that you have never drawn tears from him? [4]

The worth of the individual lies for Rousseau not in his ideas or his achievements, but in his 'sensibility'.

(*c*) Even those who are unhappy about these two gifts can still be grateful for his *insight into natural beauty*. His inability to fit into the society of the time sent him to nature for refuge. Some of the most beautiful passages in the novel to which reference has been made are those in which Saint-Preux describes the scenery around Lake Leman and the simple life of the peasantry in Canton Vaud. Nature here answers to the varying emotions in a lover's breast. Towards the end of his life, when he had withdrawn in suspicion from his fellows, nature came to mean still more to him. On the one hand, he could describe a landscape with mi-

[4] *Ibid.*, V. vi.

nute attention to detail: on the other, he could allow the power and beauty of it to sink into his being and induce a sense of peace and unity with nature.[5]

CHAPTER III   Human Nature

ROUSSEAU tells us in the *Confessions* of the intense emotional upheaval he went through at Vincennes in the summer of 1749 when he read in the *Mercure de France* that the Academy of Dijon offered a prize for an essay on: Has the progress of the sciences and arts done more to corrupt morals or to improve them? He entered the competition and was awarded the prize. Fame came to him with it as well, and in after years he dated his ruin from the decision to compete. The subject was one that suited admirably his talent for facile generalization. He drew on the classics for a description of how the societies of the ancient world lost their manly and military virtues when they began to cultivate the arts and sciences. Only the shining example of Sparta redeems the distressing picture to some extent. History is the record of man's steady deterioration from what he was in a state of nature— and he calls the result civilization and is proud of it!

There is no attempt in this first *Discourse* to describe the condition of nature. The word 'nature', to be sure, has been put to many uses, and Rousseau's use of it is as ambiguous as most. He does not yet affirm dogmatically that man was originally good. Indeed, at one point he explicitly states that "human nature was not at bottom better then than now", but he also says of the men of early times that "they were innocent and virtuous and loved to have the gods for witnesses of their actions".[6] At the close of the essay, however, he makes it clear that the common man, just because he is nearer to the state of nature than his sophisticated fellows, is morally superior to them.

[5] See the passage from *The Reveries of a Solitary Walker*, 1778 translated in *French Thought in the Eighteenth Century*, 1953, pp. 41f.
[6] *The Social Contract and Discourses*, Everyman's Library, pp. 132, 145.

Virtue! sublime science of simple minds, are such industry and preparation needed if we are to know you? Are not your principles graven on every heart? Need we do more, to learn your laws, than examine ourselves, and listen to the voice of conscience, when the passions are silent? [7]

Of much greater importance was the *Discourse on Inequality*, written for another competition organized by the same Academy, but not this time a prize-winner. In this he seeks to trace the origin of social inequality and to consider how far it is justified by natural law. His conclusion is that man is good by nature but ruined by wrong social institutions. The appendix to the *Discourse* put this in so many words.

That men are actually wicked, a sad and continual experience of them proves beyond doubt: but, all the same, I think I have shown that man is naturally good. What then can have depraved him to such an extent, except that changes that have happened in his constitution, the advances he has made, and the knowledge he has acquired? We may admire human society as much as we please; it will be none the less true that it necessarily leads men to hate each other in proportion as their interests clash, and to do one another apparent services, while they are really doing every imaginable mischief.[8]

The most perplexing feature of the analysis is that the fault seems to lie at bottom with the fact that man is man and not a mere animal. Man possesses

the faculty of self-improvement, which, by the help of circumstances, gradually develops all the rest of our faculties, and is inherent in the species as in the individual. . . . It is this faculty, which successively producing in different ages his discoveries and his errors, his vices and his virtues, makes him at length a tyrant both over himself and over nature.[9]

[7] *Ibid.*, pp. 153f.
[8] *Ibid.*, pp. 239f.
[9] *Ibid.*, p. 185.

The impulse to improve our condition is responsible for those crowning disasters, private property and the state. "Crimes, wars, and murders" were let loose on the earth by the first man who enclosed a piece of land, claimed it as his own, and excluded others from it. True, we are not to regard such an action as mere arbitrary usurpation on the part of some individual. The development of human needs and the invention of techniques to meet those needs led inevitably to such a consummation. It is as if man were fated by his intelligence to involve himself ever more deeply in misery. Once economic inequality had arisen, the possessions of the rich were in danger from the resentment of the poor. The situation produced a fraud to meet it. The rich suggested a social contract that would turn the poor into defenders of a system they might otherwise have destroyed. Under the plea of mutual advantage and common obligations, they were persuaded to surrender their liberty.

> Such was, or may well have been, the origin of society and law, which bound new fetters on the poor, and gave new powers to the rich; which irretrievably destroyed natural liberty, eternally fixed the law of property and inequality, converted clever usurpation into unalterable right, and, for the advantage of a few ambitious individuals, subjected all mankind to perpetual labour, slavery, and wretchedness.[10]

The state, as the Marxist would say, is 'the gang in power'.

This is not, and does not pretend to be, a historical sketch of how social institutions arose. It is a myth, by which Rousseau projects upon the past his disgust at the kind of society in which he lives. But what remedy does he propose for the evils he describes? Are we to abandon property, law, and the state and run wild in the woods like the noble savage? Not at all. We have contracted a disease without which we cannot now hope to live. Let us—so he argues—accept the

[10] *Ibid.*, p. 221.

society in which we find ourselves and make it at least a sphere of the private virtues, leaving it to wise rulers to palliate, prevent, or cure the evils endemic in civilization.

CHAPTER IV   Education

IT has been suggested that Rousseau had his private reasons for asserting that man is naturally good.

> He had committed wicked deeds. But since he was a natural man and Nature is good, how could Jean-Jacques be wicked? Belief in the original goodness of human nature was for him, therefore, a vital spiritual need.[11]

He returned to this thesis in the pedagogical novel *Emile*, a book that ranks with *The Social Contract* for its influence on posterity. Its starting point is that man has made vile every prospect that was meant to be pleasing, himself included.

> God makes all things good; man meddles with them and they become evil. He forces one soil to yield the products of another, one tree to bear another's fruit. He confuses and confounds time, place, and natural conditions. He mutilates his dog, his horse, and his slave. He destroys and defaces all things; he loves all that is deformed and monstrous; he will have nothing as nature made it, not even man himself, who must learn his paces like a saddle-horse, and be shaped to his master's taste like the trees in his garden.[12]

But, as in the second *Discourse*, he shrinks from what might seem the logical conclusion. He does not suggest that the child be allowed to grow up without education of any kind, since interference is sure to spoil him. He admits that society is inescapable. But

[11] F. C. Green: *Jean-Jacques Rousseau*, 1955, p. 122.
[12] *Op. cit.*, Everyman's Library, p. 5.

a 'natural' type of education is possible, one that does not impose some conventional pattern on each child but permits his self-development in freedom. Education of this kind should begin in the home and from birth. Let the mother not delegate to others the care of her child in his tender years, but rather make it her own concern. Further the extremes of neglect and of spoiling are equally to be eschewed. The child must learn to accept his environment as something to which he must adjust himself and that does not bend to his purposes. If, for example, he asks for a distant object, do not bring it to him but carry him to it. Only then will he realize that it costs effort to get it. Let him grow up neither cringing to others nor seeking to dominate them, capable of adapting himself to a range of circumstances and accepting hardship without complaint. The one habit he must be taught to form is—not having any habits!

The father, too, must play his part in the training of the child, or at least provide him with a capable tutor. We are therefore to imagine Emile growing up in charge of a single tutor, who is Rousseau himself, *plus* an establishment of servants trained to their part in the process. Two points in the programme outlined are particularly worthy of notice. The first is that each stage of life has its own standards and is not merely a preparation for the adult stage; full development as a youth is the best preparation for manhood. The second is that the pupil should be taught by the natural consequences of his acts and not by some arbitrary system of rewards and punishments. As he sows, so shall he reap. Thus he is able to learn that there are uniformities in nature and obligations towards his fellows that are defied only at his own cost. Why beat him when he breaks windows, for example? Lock him up where there are no windows to break till he learns that he must respect what belongs to other people if he wants to associate with them.

So much for education between five and twelve. From twelve to fifteen intellectual development must be catered for. This does not mean a bookish education. Rousseau would teach by things and not by signs, by contact with the environment rather than through literature. An exception is made in favour of one book, a library in itself. That is *Robinson Crusoe*. For here we are shown how a man acquires knowledge under pressure of necessity and always such knowledge as is useful to him. Learning should be a pleasure, and to that end the youth must be shown its bearing on his life here and now; he will not be touched by the argument that it will 'come in useful one day.'. Let him miss a few entertainments because he cannot read the notes of invitation, and he will master the alphabet quickly enough. Let him get lost in the woods when he is hungry, and he will follow eagerly your instructions on the points of the compass and how to find one's direction. Unfortunately, nature does not always provide the right situations, so that some have to be manufactured and these are less convincing.

We come now to moral instruction, for which reliance is placed on the presence in the pupil and indeed of every human being of an impulse that leads him to pity those who suffer or are in any need. There is too a self-love that is natural and so good; society corrupts this by placing the child in situations where he clashes with others and has to assert himself or to defer to them if he is to gain his ends. Emile has fortunately been spared such experiences. The time comes, however, when as an adolescent he needs friends and has to be helped to right relations with his fellows. He is not yet ripe for feminine society, so he must be taught to associate with young men of his own age and similar disposition. Not as though friendship were all we need. The social emotions Nature implanted in us in germ when she gave us pity must range much wider. Emile is to acquire a passion for social justice. The common man, he will learn, is the salt of the earth, and the misery to which he is reduced is the guilt of those whose social station is higher but whose moral worth is less.[13]

CHAPTER V The Social Contract

IF Rousseau is to be believed, society is responsible for the deplorable condition of civilized man. The advances effected by intelligence have been paid for with the loss

[13] Girls' education is dealt with in Book V.

of an original simplicity. Yet, as we have seen, he does not propose a return to the simple life, free from the errors and ambitions of society, but rather that we should make the best of what has come upon us. Emile is to be educated so that he can take his place in society and not be ruined by it. It would appear from this that, while man's urge to self-improvement made *some* form of society inevitable, it did not commit him to the particular type of society we have today. That is to say, a development is theoretically conceivable that would have given man the advantages of association and even of law, without requiring him to surrender his original goodness in the process. In the second *Discourse*, Rousseau had sketched a form of social contract by which the few imposed their rule on the many under the pretence of promoting the common good. Could there be a genuine form of contract, one that would actually promote the common good? "Man is born free; and everywhere he is in chains?" [14] Is there a restraint that would be legitimate and not inimical to freedom?

That is the problem Rousseau sets himself. He wants

> to find a form of association which will defend and protect with the whole common force the person and goods of each associate, and in which each, while uniting himself with all, may still obey himself alone, and remain as free as before.[15]

The solution is for each individual to put himself as it were into the common pool, thus conferring upon the whole the power it needs to protect the rights of its members, and by the same act receiving in return a guarantee that power will in fact be used for that purpose.

> Each of us puts his person and all his power in common under the supreme direction of the general will, and, in our corporate capacity, we receive each member as an indivisible part of the whole.[16]

[14] *The Social Contract* etc., p. 5.
[15] *Ibid.*, p. 14.
[16] *Ibid.*, p. 15. One is reminded of the proposals for 'collective security' between the wars.

What happens is that the individual persons combine to form a collective person, which is but themselves under a different aspect, with the result that in obeying its laws they are conforming to their own will and therefore are as free as they were before setting up the association. The sovereignty of the people gives us what is wanted.

In this account the operative term is "the general will". How is this to be defined? It is to be defined morally and not psychologically. By which is meant that it is not the will of the whole as somehow existing apart from those who compose it. It is *their* will, or rather what their will ought to be, what it becomes in so far as each considers the common good and not his own advantage. Since those who enter the society here envisaged are still in the state of original goodness, the general will is infallible. But alas, who is in that state today? The decisions taken in the societies that actually exist may claim to be for the common good, but they are often contrary to it. In these cases, Rousseau would have us speak of "the will of all" rather than of "the general will". What we have is the resultant of a clash of claims and counterclaims, not devotion to the common good. Especially does the will of all displace the general will when factions are formed within the community and each promotes its own interest.

The social contract Rousseau has described is not a historical or prehistorical event: it is a myth, the presentation of what ought to be by a story of what once was. In any case, the thesis of natural goodness appears to break down somewhere. We were told that man is good but was corrupted by society. But how, we ask, can he be corrupted within a society that so carefully excludes the factors that corrupt? Perhaps it is intelligence that is at fault. "The general will is always right, but the judgment which guides it is not always enlightened." [17] Therefore a legislator is needed. But the thesis is still not saved; it is sacrificed more drastically rather. For the legislator is a mythical figure who not merely draws up a constitution; he changes human nature, makes man over again. He can only do so by appealing to some mandate from heaven. Is not this

[17] *Ibid.*, p. 34.

tantamount to saying that no 'natural' explanation can be given of the origin of society?

If however we accept provisionally the account Rousseau offers, we go on to ask how society is governed, once it has been formed. The people is sovereign but does not govern. It elects a government with executive powers, while reserving the right to criticize and even replace it. His ideal is an aristocratic republic such as, in his view, Geneva was meant to be.

> It is the best and most natural arrangement that the wisest should govern the many, when it is assured that they will govern for its profit, and not for their own.[18]

Two questions remain to be asked. (a) How is the general will to be ascertained? In practice, we are told, by a majority vote. For, if each person votes according to what he honestly thinks to be the common good and finds himself in the minority, this of itself shows that he was mistaken, so that to accept the decision of the majority is to accept the common good. The will of the majority, if not preverted by self- or group-interest (how serious these 'ifs' are!), will disclose and express the general will. (b) What happens to a recalcitrant citizen, one who stubbornly adheres to an opinion not shared by the majority? He "will be forced to be free".[19] If we object, Rousseau will reply that by this he means simply that such a person is guilty of a breach of the original contract and must be punished therefor.

CHAPTER VI   Religion

It only remains now to pick up a loose thread from each of the two preceding sections. Emile's tutor, we saw, undertook his moral training. For his religious training he calls in an expert, whom he introduces as a Savoyard vicar. The vicar gives an account of his doubts

[18] *Ibid.*, pp. 60f.
[19] *Ibid.*, p. 18.

and how he arrived at faith, a faith that was denounced in unmeasured terms by the Archbishop of Paris. It is in fact a vague theism, as indulgent to the emotions as it is sparing in its demands on the intellect. Appeal is made neither to revelation nor, except in a subordinate sense, to reasoning, but to the heart, or, in Rousseau's expression, to an inner feeling. For "to perceive is to feel",[20] and the divine is accessible only through feeling. But, if Rousseau is in opposition to the dogmas of Catholicism, he is equally hostile to the atheism and cynicism of so many of the *philosophes*. Reflection convinces him, as it does the vicar, that there is a great First Cause, and this he identifies with the God whom he apprehends by feeling.

This being who wills and can perform his will, this being active through his own power, this being, whoever he may be, who moves the universe and orders all things, is what I call God. To this name I add the ideas of intelligence, power, will, which I have brought together, and that of kindness which is their necessary consequence; but for all this I know no more of the being to which I ascribe them.[21]

The problem of evil costs the vicar no sleepless nights. Moral evil is due to man's freedom, physical evil is largely the result of our disregard of nature's wise order. The soul's immortality is not to be questioned; the inequalities of this life cry out for another in which its wrongs will be redressed. The reward that awaits the virtuous after death is apparently the highest form of self-satisfaction, "that pure delight which springs from self-content".[22] Petitionary prayer is dismissed as unworthy. The vicar reveres Christ, but finds not a little in the New Testament of which he cannot approve. The one inspired book God has given is nature and the one true religion is that of the heart. Nevertheless, he conforms to what the Church demands of him.

Rousseau has given us a natural religion that differs from most others because it appeals to the emotions rather than the intellect. In substance it was present already in the dying Julie's confession in *La Nouvelle*

[20] *Emile*, p. 232.
[21] *Ibid.*, p. 239.
[22] *Ibid.*, p. 246.

Héloïse and in *Emile* he gives it a larger part in the education of woman than in that of man.

In *The Social Contract,* as might be expected, interest shifts from private to public religion. Where is his society to find this? In Christianity, perhaps. Hardly, Rousseau would say. For Christianity, according to him, exists under two forms, one too noxious and the other too mild to be serviceable for this purpose. We need not pause over his strictures on Catholicism; his criticism of the Christianity of the Gospels is more important. It is other-worldly and teaches men to sit loose to earthly attachments because their treasure is laid up for them in heaven. Of what use is such a religion to a state that has to maintain itself against other states, by force if necessary? No doubt, it is "holy, sublime, and real". No doubt, if accepted, it would make all men brothers and rid us of every ill. But one thing it would not do; it would not brace them to make and maintain a free community, if necessary at the cost of their lives. It is strange indeed to find a scion of Swiss Calvinism writing that

> Christianity preaches only servitude and dependence. Its spirit is so favourable to tyranny that it always profits by such a regime. True Christians are made to be slaves, and they know it and do not much mind: this short life counts for too little in their eyes.[23]

There must therefore be a civil religion, the dogmas of which are decided upon by the sovereign people. Should they not rather be prescribed by the legislator who founds the society in the name of the gods?

> The dogmas of civil religion ought to be few, simple, and exactly worded, without explanation or commentary. The existence of a mighty, intelligent and beneficent Divinity, possessed of foresight and providence, the life to come, the happiness of the just, the punishment of the wicked, the sanctity of the social contract and its laws: these are its positive dogmas. Its negative dogmas I confine to one, in-

[23] *Op. cit.,* p. 120.

tolerance, which is part of the cults we have rejected.[24]

It looks as though the sovereign people had graciously voted to make Rousseau's private religion that of the state! They condemn intolerance, we are told. Excellent. But then what are we to make of the passage that precedes the one just quoted?

> If any one, after publicly recognizing these dogmas, behaves as if he does not believe them, let him be punished by death: he has committed the worst of all crimes, that of lying before the law.

Such a sentence reveals the change that had to come over men's thinking to make toleration possible. They had to grasp a possibility that eluded even Rousseau, the possibility that men might differ fundamentally on religion and still be united as citizens.

But Rousseau here confronts us with an awkward problem. We say today that democracy needs the support of a faith. Is this to be Christianity? If so, which of the rival forms of Christianity? And is Christianity really compatible with war? So we fall back on vague talk about 'spiritual values'. What is this but civil religion of a sort? One item in its creed, if we may use such a term, is certainly tolerance. But what is to be our attitude towards those who reject this creed and would destroy democracy? How far is it possible to tolerate the intolerant, to give liberty to the enemies of liberty? We are treading on dangerous ground, but Rousseau had reached it before us.

For further reading:

Translations of *Confessions, Emile, Social Contract,* and *Reveries of a Solitary Walker.*
    F. C. Green: *Jean-Jacques Rousseau.*

[24] *Ibid.,* p. 121.

PART NINE

MARX

CHAPTER I   Hegel and the Hegelians

THE influence of Rousseau was not confined to France.
It reached even to Königsberg, to the austere genius
of Kant, who has left on record that he learned from
Rousseau the worth of the common man. The common
man had other champions than writers of books and at
the French Revolution they sprang to arms in his cause,
at first literally and then metaphorically. Enthusiasts
like Tom Paine firmly believed that events in France,
the overthrow of the monarchy and the entry of the
people upon their rights, would bring in a new era for
all mankind. Soon, however, it began to appear that
the revolution had effected no more than a transfer of
power from the aristocracy to the middle class and that
more desperate measures were needed if the common
man was really to profit by the change. Francis Noel
Babeuf (1764-1797) is cited today as the first communist. His creed ran: "The aim of society is the happiness
of all, and happiness consists in equality".[1]

Contemporaneously with the French Revolution, a
succession of German philosophers developed what
Kant had begun, sometimes in agreement with him but
more often in criticism. Of these the greatest was Hegel.
He could not accept the Kantian surrender to ignorance
in face of things-in-themselves; the human mind must
penetrate and subdue even their world. Nor was he interested in physics as Kant had been. He belonged to
a historically minded generation. He saw his own philosophy, for example, as the culminating point in a development that began with the Greeks, and he was
largely responsible for the creation of new disciplines

[1] Quoted in Harry W. Laidler: *A History of Socialist
Thought,* 1933, p. 57.

such as the philosophy of history and the philosophy of religion.

But how grapple with history? The old logic, derived from Aristotle, was inadequate. For it was concerned with what *is*, while in history one watches how one thing *becomes* another. How grasp and articulate change? Hegel had his method and he called it dialectic. It was not his invention, of course, for it went back to the Greeks. The word suggests a dialogue and it will be helpful to consider how a dialogue often works out. I state a case A, you point out its defects and argue for B, and as a result of the discussion we reach C, which does justice to what was true in both positions while discarding what we now agree was mistaken. Or one may run through just such a three-stage process in one's own mind. On Hegel's view, this is how history develops. It begins with a *thesis,* over against which as one-sided the *antithesis* emerges; both then contribute towards the final *synthesis.* That however is not the end, for C is seen to be defective, and so the whole process starts over again.

So, in politics, a government of the Left goes too far in control by the state, whereupon the electorate replaces it by one from the Right with a mandate to restore individual liberties. That goes too far and eventually a balance is reached. This, to be sure, is unstable, and the effort to reach a satisfactory social pattern continues. For Hegel history is a process in which man wins freedom. Among the Oriental nations, one person, the despot, was free and the rest were his slaves. Among the Greeks and Romans, some were free and the rest slaves. Now, the Germanic people have reached the stage at which all are free. Similarly, in the *Philosophy of Religion,* we pass from the religion of nature to the religion of individual spirituality and so to Christianity as the absolute religion.

But we now take a bolder step. The dialetical process is not merely at work in conversation, history, and religion. Hegel extends it beyond these and so doing consciously transforms it. These partial processes are but phases of one ultimate and all-inclusive process that cannot be observed but can only be grasped by thought. The development of mind and history reflect that ultimate development in the course of which mind and history come to be. The Absolute Spirit realizes itself

151

through a movement of thesis, antithesis, and synthesis whereof nature and man, the individual and society, science and morality, art and religion are the necessary stages. Each contributes something to the movement and so to the fulness of the Absolute Spirit, which is not to be thought of as apart from them, but only as in and through them. The absolute process is therefore not historical and not in time; for it is that of which history and time are aspects.

This is the Absolute Idealism of Hegel, and it captured the German mind in its day. It yields two widely divergent sets of practical conclusions, however. If, on the one hand, you regard the existing state of things as the climax of a long development, enriched by the gains of centuries, then your duty will be to maintain the *status quo* in Church and State. For is not this the goal the Absolute Spirit has reached in its self-development? That was the position of the Right Hegelians. On the other hand, since the dialectical process is interminable, you may regard the existing state of things as inherently defective and requiring to be superseded by one more satisfactory. In which case, you will work for a change in religion and politics. That was the position of the Left Hegelians. One of these greatly influenced Marx, and to him we now turn.

CHAPTER II   Beyond Feuerbach

LUDWIG FEUERBACH (1804-1872) told the story of his intellectual pilgrimage in the sentence: "God was my first thought, reason my second, man my first and last". In other words, he began from Christianity, went through a Hegelian phase, and arrived at humanism, even at materialism of a kind. His criticism of Hegel was both shrewd and sound. He saw in Hegelianism a secularized and diluted version of Christian theology.

The Absolute Spirit is only the 'departed spirit' of theology, which still goes about like a ghost in the Hegelian philosophy.[2]

[2] *Werke*, 1846, Vol. II, p. 249.

The grand error of Hegel was that he imagined thinking could of itself give access to reality. Did he not say that "the real is the rational, and the rational is the real"? But this is to turn matters upside down. What *is* takes precedence of what we *think*; indeed, it determines what we think. So Feuerbach averred that "thought is the product of being, and not being of thought".[3] What is meant by 'being' in this case? Man in his concrete actuality, man rooted in nature and the sense-world, however he may rise above them.

This is what is meant by Feuerbach's notorious aphorism: "Man is what he eats". The flights of speculation are not possible where one's bodily needs claim all one's attention. His own standpoint, he said, was neither idealism nor materialism, but anthropology. Hence that other slogan of his: "Theology is anthropology". That is to say, all statements about God are meaningless when taken as applicable to a Being other than man; they become rich in meaning when translated into statements about man. This is the thesis developed in his *Essence of Christianity* (1841), which George Eliot was to translate into English. Religion, so the argument runs, is the product of fantasy-thinking: what we aspire to for ourselves we predicate of God. He is dressed out in the clothes we should like to order for ourselves, but that we know simply would not fit us. We call him infinite, eternal, omnipotent, because we should love to be all those things ourselves. We compensate for our shortcomings by imagining them all supplied in him, and then we fall down and worship him.

But what makes us project these fantasies upon God instead of enjoying self-dramatization for its own sake? When we imagine man all-powerful or all-loving, it is not ourselves as individuals that we transform in this way, but human nature, the humanity common to us and all men. Now humanity and the race transcend our brief life; they were here before us and will be here after us. It is easy therefore to mistake them for a Being other than ourselves, God. The history of religion is the history of man's various idealizations of himself. So long as we distinguish between the one who idealizes and what is idealized, the illusion

3 *Ibid.*, p. 263.

of religion remains. Once we see through the illusion, religion vanishes. And Christianity has made this insight possible for us. Its doctrine of the Incarnation has betrayed the secret. God, we are told, became man. We know what that means. Man has become God, has realized that he is the only 'God' there is. Now that the truth is out, man must become his own saviour. He must do in actuality what he has been doing in fantasy for so long. But be it remembered that 'man' is ambiguous. The truth for the future is that social man must redeem individual man.

We see at once what such a train of thought had to offer to Marx.[4] His *Theses on Feuerbach,* found by Engels in an old notebook and published after his colleague's death, contain the germ of much that was to develop later. At two points he learned from Feuerbach even while he differed from him.

In the first place, Feuerbach's anthropology is not concrete enough. He "resolves the religious essence into the human", and in that he is right for Marx. But his account of the human essence is too abstract. He thinks in terms of humanity and the race. But do these in fact exist? Is not man, as Hegel saw, a historical being through and through? Does not that mean that man exists only as member of a society with a particular social and economic structure? Again, Feuerbach was right in stressing that man is a sensuous being and not merely a thinking one; but the senses are not for contemplation but for action. Man is a being who constructs, maintains, and overthrows particular forms of society. If therefore collective man is to be the saviour of individual man, will it not be as a socially active collectivity, as a revolutionary class, that he will do this?

In the second place, Feuerbach was right to uncover the wishful thinking that lies behind all religion. Man turns to a god of his own creation because he is dissatisfied with himself, has needs he cannot meet. But why not carry the analysis a stage further and ask precisely what these needs are that give rise to religion? Are they those that inhere in a particular form of society rather than in anything so vague as human nature? If so, then the way to undercut religion is not by a psychological

---

[4] Freud's debt to Feuerbach is equally clear.

analysis but by removing what is wrong in the social structure.

> Thus, for instance, once the earthly family is discovered to be the secret of the holy family, the former must then itself be theoretically criticized and radically changed in practice.[5]

The principle that theory and practice must be one had appeared already in Feuerbach, but Marx extends it. The problems that confront us must be both analyzed and tackled, and the two processes should go on side by side, each helping the other. "The philosophers have only *interpreted* the world in various ways; the point however is to change it."[6]

CHAPTER III   The Theory of Value

WHAT now was the situation with which Marx was called upon to deal, both by interpreting it and by changing it? It was that created by capitalist industrialism as he saw it first in the Rhineland, where he grew up, and subsequently in England, where he lived so long as an exile. The theory he embodied in his great work *Capital* was worked out before he arrived in London, but it is supported there by evidence supplied in part by Engels and in part by the official reports stored in the reading room of the British Museum. Engels, his devoted colleague and financial supporter, had interests in the Lancashire cotton-industry and after Marx's death wrote in 1892 on *The Condition of the Working Class in England in 1844*. The picture to be put together from these various sources was frightening in the extreme: women and children worn out by long hours of labour, wages cut to a minimum, wretched housing conditions, disease and ignorance. Yet some grew rich under these conditions and pleaded 'not guilty' to the charge of exploiting their workers. The fault, they said, lay with

---

[5] Emile Burns: *A Handbook of Marxism*, 1936, p. 230.
[6] *Ibid.*, p. 231.

155

the nature of the economic system, the law of supply and demand.

Earlier Socialists and radicals had reacted to such a plea with moral indignation. There was something of this in the young Marx, when he was a Hegelian of the Left. He used the language of Idealism then, writing of how man had become "alienated from himself" under capitalism and how it was time to end this unhappy condition. As we should express it, capitalism had brought about 'the dehumanization of man' and he must now be restored to his proper dignity. But, as he grew older, he scorned the Utopian Socialism that had come down from the left wing of the French Revolution after Babeuf and that in some cases actually appealed to the New Testament. He meant to replace this by a Socialism that was through and through scientific and therefore effective. It would avoid moral judgments and would aim simply at an accurate diagnosis as guide to the drastic operation that would prove necessary. Hence he set aside the appeal to the brotherhood of man that was current among working-class reformers of his day, substituting for it a summons to the outraged proletariat to revolt. He lived at a time when change was being demanded in most countries of Western Europe, when even England was astir with Chartism. If only he could capture these movements!

The scientific Socialism he propounded was half economics and half philosophy of history. We shall be concerned in this section with the former. John Locke had already argued that labour is the source of economic value. A man "mixes his labour" with what nature supplies freely and the result has value both for use and exchange. Ricardo, though he had no quarrel with capitalism, exposed its ugliness when he argued that the exchange value of a commodity is determined by the labour needed to produce it, while the wage paid to the worker is the minimum necessary to keep him alive and enable him to produce children who will one day become workers in their turn. One is left wondering what becomes of the difference between the two amounts. It is the source of the employer's wealth. It is not contended here that Ricardo's analysis is sound, but only that it was taken up by Marx and used to demonstrate that capitalism is sheer exploitation.

The principle he lays down is that

that which determines the magnitude of the value of any article is the amount of labour socially necessary, or the labour-time socially necessary for its production. . . . The value of one commodity is to the value of any other, as the labour-time necessary for the production of the one is to that necessary for the production of the other. 'As values, all commodities are only definite masses of congealed labour-time." [7]

But—and here is the snag for the industrial worker—under capitalism the worker owns neither tools nor materials. These belong to the capitalist who hires his labour, the one commodity he does possess. The latter hires him outright to work, let us say, ten hours a day. If we simplify the matter in crude fashion to make clear what happens (for Marx, of course), we may suppose that at the end of seven hours the worker has produced enough to support himself and family. Does the employer then tell him to go home? Not at all. He pays him that as his wage—and keeps him working for three more hours. During that period the worker produces what Marx calls surplus value. This accrues to the capitalist, who can spend it or invest it in business to keep the lucrative process going indefinitely.

There is only one word for this procedure. It is exploitation. But let us not get morally indignant about it or blame the individual capitalist. He may be kind-hearted, a good husband and father, a faithful church-man, and so on, much superior to many of his employees. It is the system that is at fault and not the individuals who work it. So that word 'exploitation' must be taken in a strictly technical and objective sense, as when we speak of exploiting the natural resources of a country. What Marx is dealing with are individuals as "personifications of economic categories, embodiments of particular class-relations and class-interests". [8] No doubt, he aims at being severely objective. Yet there seems to be a moral judgment implicit in his analysis. This comes out particularly in what he has to say of the "fetishism of commodities". Instead of

---

[7] *Ibid.*, p. 409. 'Socially necessary' because, e.g., more time is taken by a craftsman than a machine-minder, so that the product is cheaper in the second case.

[8] *Capital*, 1920, p. xix.

goods being produced to meet the needs of persons, they are produced as a means of making money and persons are organized to make and buy them. "Things are in the saddle and rule mankind." So a whole system develops in which men and women feel themselves subject to anonymous and inaccessible powers. A man is thrown out of work and his family goes hungry because the price of rubber has gone up or down, he knows not why.

CHAPTER IV   Dialectical Materialism

IN his home at Trier near Bonn the young Marx had been brought up in the ideals of the eighteenth century, its belief in education, in progress, and in the perfectibility of human nature. Then he had been fascinated by the Hegelian philosophy, history as the drama the Absolute enacts before itself as spectator. But already in the eighteenth century another influence was at work, a materialism that sometimes allied itself with the enthusiasms of the time and sometimes mocked at them. It was a scientific materialism, and it was gaining ground in Germany as Marx grew up. All these influences blended in his thought as he came to maturity, so that in him materialism, without retracting its claim to be scientific, became historical in Hegelian fashion and at the same time an instrument of social change. He saw the material aspect of human life, not in its physical environment, but in its economic conditions. Not Absolute Spirit, not the Idea, is the genius that presides over history, but the system of production.

In the emphasis thus laid on economic factors he had of course been anticipated by others. Nevertheless, it was he who forced on posterity a full recognition of the part they play. For him, they were primary and everything else secondary, deriving therefrom such importance and power as they possessed. Society resembles a great building, the foundations and ground floor of which are provided by economic forces, so that nothing can be built on it that does not conform to their pattern. The words in which he expresses this conception are so weighty that they must be quoted in full.

> The mode of production of the material means of existence conditions the whole process of social, political, and intellectual life. It is not the consciousness of men that determines their existence, but, on the contrary, it is their social existence that determines their consciousness.[9]

Is not this to turn Hegel upside down? Yes, and Marx meant to do precisely that. Yet we shall see that he remains a Hegelian even when he flouts the master.

Hegel taught that each period, each nation has its own peculiar character that comes to expression in its institutions, its art, its philosophy, etc. Marx agreed, but he sought the distinctive feature of a period in its economic system, since man's basic needs are food, clothing, and shelter. One of the best presentations of this view of society and its many activities is that of Nikolai Bukharin in his *Historical Materialism*. He seeks to show how the political structure of a historical period, its science and art, its religion and philosophy are but so many functions of its productive system. Thus, the impulse to scientific development is not to be found in a disinterested desire to know the truth, but in the pressure of need.

> The following principle is of fundamental importance: every science is born from practice, from the conditions and needs of the struggle for life on the part of social man with nature, and of the various social groups, with the elemental forces of society or with other groups.[10]

In a slave society like that of ancient Athens, manual labour was despised and education was either for the civic duties that devolved on the free citizen or for the conversation and speculation in which he spent the leisure he enjoyed at the expense of his slaves. Medieval society extended the hierarchical principle from land-tenure to philosophy and even to religion. God was approached through the saints as intermediaries, whereas

[9] Burns: *Op. cit.*, p. 372.
[10] *Op. cit.*, 1925, p. 161.

in bourgeois society every man claims the right of direct access to him. Capitalism glorifies the vigorous and energetic personality, attaches value to the useful, and finds a sanction for imperial expansion in evangelical zeal.

Such is the picture we see when we look at each phase of social development by itself. But how do we pass from one phase to the next? Here again the decisive factor is the economic one and the pattern of the process is the Hegelian dialectic in this new, materialist version. A given society is the thesis that contains its own antithesis within itself. The system of production outgrows the social and political forms amid which it has developed. They were its kindly nurse at birth, but they threaten to stifle it now it has reached maturity.

> At a certain stage of their development the material productive forces of society come into contradiction with the existing productive relationships, or, what is but a legal expression for these, with the property relationships within which they had moved before. From forms of development of the productive forces these relationships are transformed into their fetters. Then an epoch of social revolution opens. With a change in the economic foundation the whole vast superstructure is more or less rapidly transformed.[11]

Thus, the Industrial Revolution brought into being a middle class that broke through the restraints imposed by a society based on the ownership of land. So doing, it changed not only the social structure but also the pattern of family relations; it introduced new standards in art and new moral ideals. But the change was possible only because it had long been preparing. The old system had exhausted its possibilities and the new had developed to the point at which it could take over.

> A social system never perishes before all the productive forces have developed for which it is wide enough; and new, higher productive relationships never come into being before the material conditions

[11] Burns: *Op. cit.*, p. 372.

for their existence have been brought to maturity within the womb of the old society itself. Therefore mankind always sets itself only such problems as it can solve; for when we look closer we will always find that the problem itself only arises when the material conditions for its solution are already present or at least in process of coming in to being.[12]

Marx was convinced that the hour of destiny had arrived for the capitalist society built up by the middle class in Western Europe. History is moving towards revolution and the only rational course is to move with it. The iron is glowing. Watch for the moment to strike!

CHAPTER V   Class War

HEGEL has said that "the knowledge of necessity is freedom", and Marx agreed with him. That is to say, once we know the laws that govern the historical process, we know how to act upon it and change it. Marxism is not therefore determinist in the sense that nothing can happen otherwise than it in fact does. A certain end is bound to be achieved, but man can facilitate or obstruct the achievement for a time. Often, no doubt, he struggles for immediate interests only, as when workers strike for an increase of pay. Theorists like Marx are needed to extend his horizon. By making him fully conscious of what is happening and what is at stake, they enable him to participate intelligently in shaping the future out of the present. Others before Marx had recognized in history tension and conflict between classes, each of which represents some specific interest. Marx elaborated the explanation, demonstrating—at least to his own satisfaction—that the laws of the struggle are those of war, and throwing himself on the side of one class, the proletariat.

The historical materialism of the preceding section brought out how in each period of history the few batten on the many. All other distinctions within a so-

12 *Ibid.*, pp. 372f.

ciety are trivial in comparison with that between the exploited who create surplus value and the exploiters who appropriate it. As the *Communist Manifesto* puts it:

> The history of all hitherto existing society is the history of class struggles.
>
> Freeman and slave, patrician and plebeian, lord and serf, guild-master and journeyman, in a word, oppressor and oppressed, stood in constant opposition to one another, carried on an uninterrupted, now hidden, now open fight, a fight that each time ended, either in a revolutionary reconstruction of society at large, or in the common ruin of the contending classes.[13]

Here again we must learn not to pass moral judgments. In earlier stages of development advance would not have been possible in a less cruel way. For example, the bourgeoisie was historically necessary if the rigidities of the feudal system were to be broken down, if distant lands were to be linked by transport, and if production was to be developed to the point at which it would support a higher standard of living all round. The capitalist middle class must be abolished, not at all because it is wicked, but because it is out of date. It has fulfilled its task and now stands in the way of further progress.

Of course, the oppressed class does not take this detached view of what is happening. That it should not is again historically necessary, for it is being prepared for a revolutionary role. It feels the impact of power from above and resents its own suffering and humiliation. It therefore begins with complaint and goes on finally to revolt. To be sure, the struggle is not always as overt and acknowledged as this analysis would seem to imply. Each of the contending classes fabricates an ideology that serves at once as a weapon in its struggle for power and as a smoke-screen concealing from itself and others the naked reality of the struggle.

In considering such revolutions it is always necessary to distinguish between the material revolution

[13] *Ibid.*, pp. 22f.

in the economic conditions of production, which can be determined with scientific accuracy, and the judicial, political, religious, aesthetic or philosophic— in a word, ideological forms wherein men become conscious of this conflict and fight it out.[14]

So the possessors appeal to law and order, the dispossessed to human rights; the middle class develops an ethic of individual liberty and brands the closed shop as tyranny, the working class develops an ethic of solidarity, with trade unions, friendly societies, and co-operative societies as its expression. The squire goes to the parish church, the labourer to the local chapel. There are no common standards but only those that serve each class in its struggle. They both speak of justice, but they do not mean the same thing by it. There is bourgeois justice, which guarantees the position of the property-owner, and there is proletarian justice, which aims at a more equitable distribution of wealth. There is no standard by which it can be said that one of these approaches is right and the other wrong. Marx would claim, however, that the time comes when one can be seen to be outdated and the other to have the future with it.

Hitherto, the struggle has been waged each time only to be begun all over again when the issue has apparently been decided. The new class that takes over from the exploiters turns exploiter itself, and so the process goes on. But not for ever. Capitalism has created a new and final situation. Its progress has two effects. First, in its insatiable lust for profit it depresses the condition of the workers more and more, and at the same time squeezes out the various groups between capitalists and proletariat; all alike sink deeper in the mire. Second, large-scale industry brings the workers together in trade unions, gives them the measure of education needed for their tasks, and thus recruits and drills the army that is to storm the capitalist fortress. There must be no precipitate action, to be sure, no bomb-throwing in the streets. There must be discipline. Wait till the time is ripe and then take over.

The advance of industry, whose involuntary pro-

14 *Ibid.*, p. 372.

moter is the bourgeoisie, replaces the isolation of the labourers, due to competition, by their revolutionary combination, due to association. The development of modern industry, therefore, cuts from under its feet the very foundation on which the bourgeoisie produces and appropriates products. What the bourgeoisie therefore produces, above all, are its own grave-diggers. Its fall and the victory of the proletariat are equally inevitable.[15]

This will be something that goes beyond all previous revolutions. For by this time the issue has been simplified to one between the few with their flaunting wealth and all the rest in their misery, now grown intolerable.

Let the ruling classes tremble at a Communist revolution. The proletarians have nothing to lose but their chains. They have a world to win.
Working men of all countries, unite! [16]

It is quite out of the question that the workers should do what their predecessors did, and turn exploiters once they have power in their hands. And that for the simple reason that there will be no one to exploit. They are the last class and after them the millenium. The society they will introduce will be classless; because there were only two classes left and now one of these has liquidated the other. For the first time it makes sense to speak of a universal human morality. For a while, to be sure, the proletariat will rule through a strong state of its own type that will nationalize the means of production, step up education, and organize for maximum production. But one day the state will wither away in the new climate created by these measures and

in place of the old bourgeois society, with its classes and class antagonisms, we shall have an association in which the free development of each is the condition for the free development of all.[17]

[15] *Ibid.*, p. 36.
[16] *Ibid.*, p. 59.
[17] *Ibid.*, p. 47.

IT is clear that there is a religious quality about all this. The attitude of the Communist is strikingly similar to that of the Calvinist. Each is convinced that the power behind history is on his side, the economic process in the one case and God's predestination on the other. Yet neither allows the certainty of final victory to impair the will to organize now and to act when the time for action comes. There is a delicate balance between man's responsibility and God's—or history's—grace. There is something religious too about the hope of ultimate deliverance; the classless society is a secularized form of the Kingdom of God. What is the class war, too, but the uncertain human conflict raised to the level of an absolute, of the war between good and evil, God and Satan? It is as a mixture of science and faith that Marxism appeals. From the first, its instrument was the political party. Marx set to work, whether in Paris, in Brussels, or in London, to organize the groups of Socialists that he found in being into a disciplined organization that would be under his control. It was for the Communist League that he wrote the *Manifesto*: theory must be sound that action might be effective.

His ambitions seemed likely to be realized when he took over the International Working Men's Association. This grew out of a meeting between French and British workers in London at the time of the 1863 Exhibition. Invitations were addressed by it to working men's associations in several countries. Let them co-operate to form an international organization with definitely socialist objectives. Marx came on the executive as representing the German artisans in London, and it only needed two meetings to enable him to dominate it. He drew up the constitution and delivered the inaugural address. The First International, as it came to be called, had a life of only thirteen years; it foundered on the hostility between Marx and Bakunin. The latter was a Russian anarchist who admired Marx for his intellectual power but detested any appeal to the state. The state must be destroyed and its place taken by a confederation of voluntary associations for economic and other purposes. While it lasted, however, the International served to establish the name of Marx as 'the red terrorist doctor' who plotted the subversion of public order, religion, and the family.

Two main schools of thought today claim for their policies the authority of Marx. There were in his thought both evolutionary and revolutionary elements; Social Democracy continues the first tendency, Communism the second. British Labour is to be brought under neither of these heads, for its inspiration is rather from the New Testament than from *Das Kapital*. The outsider may be disposed to say that neither of the two schools of thought is literally faithful to the master, that indeed literal fidelity would be foolish, since conditions have changed so greatly since his day. Each of them represents an adaptation to a new situation.

What Social Democracy builds on is the extension of the franchise and the formation of political parties able to make a bid for power within a parliamentary system. On Marx's principle that the effective blow can only be struck at the right moment, political advance by consitutional means will either create the most favourable situation for revolution or will make victory possible without it. The Communist, on the other hand, accuses the Socialist of allowing himself to be bought off by minor capitalist concessions.

Lenin's contributions to Marxist theory were the most notable ones. He recognized that capitalism had not developed as Marx thought it would, along international lines, but had allied itself with nationalism. The result was imperialism, which he defined as "the monopoly stage of capitalism",[18] the stage, that is, at which the division of the world between colonial powers had been carried right through, and no further gains were possible except by war between the rivals. And war would create, at least in the defeated country, a situation of which the party could take advantage. Here we come to Lenin's second major contribution. He wanted and created an élite of politically conscious and disciplined persons vowed to revolutionary action who would seize power when the moment came and

[18] *Ibid.*, p. 689.

exercise a dictatorship on behalf of the proletariat, crushing ruthlessly any opposition that favoured the old regime. With this we pass from ideas to history.

For further reading:

Translations of Marx, Engels, and Lenin.
E. Burns: *Handbook of Marxism.*
I. Berlin: *Karl Marx.*
H. J. Laski: *Communism.*
H. W. Laidler: *A History of Socialist Thought.*

PART TEN

NIETZSCHE

CHAPTER I   Decadence

THE Communist Manifesto is at once an analysis of the past and a tirade against the present. Marx and Engels, however, were not the only voices to be raised in protest against the bourgeois society of the mid-nineteenth century; there were others who were just as incensed and as unrestrained in their denunciation. Two in particular have become a power in our day. Kierkegaard called for a radical Christianity, a clean break with all acceptance of the *status quo* and the play-acting of a 'geographical Christianity', even should this sacrifice the continuance of the human race. He died in a Copenhagen hospital, his strength worn out by self-imposed sufferings. Nietzsche's position among the three is a peculiar one. While he agreed with their diagnoses to no slight extent, he emphatically rejected the remedies they offered. Indeed, he saw in the Social-ist movement of his day just such a revolt of the many against the few, the contemptible against the noble, as in the rise of Christianity. In all three men there was the same over-emphasis and lack of charity, the same strident confusion of personal grievance and prophetic rebuke.

Nietzsche did not doubt that Europe was in the throes of a crisis and that Germany, his own country, was at the centre of that crisis. His life spanned the period 1844-1900 that saw the meteoric rise of Ger-many, under Prussian leadership, to a position of su-premacy on the Continent. He was a mere child when the attempted revolution of 1848 ended in failure, to be replaced by Bismarck's policy of blood and iron. In a succession of campaigns, this reduced Prussia's rivals to weakness or, in the case of Austria, secured them as allies. The Empire that acclaimed a Hohenzollern as its first head entered the race with industrial countries like Britain and threatened to outstrip them. Her cities were adorned—or disfigured!—with monuments celebrating the new achievements. Her universities added the triumphs of culture to those of arms and industry. Culture! here was the point of Nietzsche's criticism. For, as he saw it, in gaining so much, Germany had lost all that mattered. No longer the land of Hölderlin and Goethe, she had become soulless and self-satisfied, substituting knowledge for wisdom, rich in possessions but miserably poor within, her scholars mere pedants, her standards those of the Philistine and her virtues those of the Pharisee.

This is not, of course, an objective account of conditions in Germany at that time. We can no more look to Nietzsche for such than we can accept Kierkegaard's broadsheets as an accurate picture of Danish church life. Both of them declared that all along the line the third-rate was triumphant, and nothing was acceptable save as it pandered to the taste of the mass. The new alarming phenomenon of the time was the journalist, who was free to say what he pleased while shielding himself from criticism by anonymity, and who debased the currency of language that he might purchase popular favour with it. The word that best suited the cultural situation as Nietzsche saw it was 'decadence'. The spurious had come to be substituted for the genuine, standards had gone by the board, and Europe was sinking into a condition in which nothing great would be possible. For society needs an élite that will set a pattern and curb the thoughtlessness of the mass. The principal characteristic of the time was its rejection of the aristocratic principle, the 'revolt of the masses' as Ortega y Gasset was to call it. The common man could not endure the rebuke of superior ability.

But the crux of his analysis was that Europe had long since turned against Christianity but still lacked the courage to confess that it had done so. It therefore continued to pay lip-service to it as an ideal while actually governing its life by quite other considerations. With Kierkegaard—and, as we have seen, with Rousseau—he held that a genuine Christianity cannot mix with the values of secular society. It calls to renunciation and not to gain, to self-denial and not to self-assertion, to forgiveness and not to the maintenance of one's rights. How much longer is the sham to continue by which the state patronizes the Church and the prosperous business man has his children confirmed so as not to interfere with their prospects? Christianity now turns against itself. It prized truth and sincerity, and truth and sincerity now require us to say exactly where we stand. We are Christians no longer.

How are we to judge of all this? It is clear at once that many of Nietzsche's criticisms of his time are precisely those that are brought against our own day. Are we to think of him as a prophetic soul whose insight discerned already the flaws in a structure that to everyone else was imposing and unquestionably secure? Or is it merely that his private resentments chime in with the pathological features of a post-war mentality? The reader is left to his own judgment.

But there can be no doubt that Nietzsche thought of himself as something of a prophet. A special responsibility devolved on him as called to face a crisis and devise means to overcome it. He felt himself to be an exception, one sundered from his fellows, marked out for a fate peculiarly his own and disciplined by suffering for the work he had to do. His career ended in a mental breakdown and towards the end he spoke of himself in preposterously fantastic terms. In his greatest work he dramatized himself as the Persian prophet Zarathustra. He felt that he had a mission to his time. He must rouse it from its lethargy, expose the hollowness of its pretensions and the self-deception of its virtues. If he was a destroyer rather than a creator, he would have said that was because the time needed such a one. But he sought to destroy existing standards only that room might be found for new and better ones.

THERE are those whose thought can be considered in isolation from their lives, but Nietzsche is not one of them. Indeed, it would not be difficult to explain his thinking as but a vast rationalization of his personal struggles. Janko Lavrin has thrown considerable light on Nietzsche's development as a continuous effort on his part to overcome the ill health from which he suffered and that proved at last too strong for him.[1] He compensated for physical disabilities by a supreme endeavour in the realm of the spirit. Above all, he saw his one hope in a deliberate affirmation of life. He must exalt it to the highest place in his scale of values, he must reject all that impaired the will-to-live, whatever attraction might attend it. On this view, the vehemence of his language betrays the fact that he is fighting against that in himself of which he is afraid. Compassion for the suffering and unfortunate was a luxury in which he could not dare to indulge. Instead, he must affirm strength, sheer brute force and vigour, since these were what he lacked and needed most.

In what follows, I shall take this summons, addressed both to his readers and to himself, to say 'Yes' to life as the key to his thought. The decadence he found in the culture of his time—what was it but an acceptance, even a cultivation, of the forces that work for the slow destruction of life, the sickly rather than the healthy, the feminine as against the masculine? Nietzsche opposed it in the name of life. But he opposed it also in the name of truth, because it was through and through insincere. How then did he relate these two values, truth and life? There are times when he sees in the unconditional demand of truth a last relic of Christian piety; man must serve truth as he once served God, and must do so even if it robs him of happiness. At other times he seems to regard truth as subordinate to life; to say that something is hostile to life is *ipso facto* to brand it as false. From this

[1] *Friedrich Nietzsche An Approach*, 1948.

second point of view, to philosophize is to experiment. One puts out certain suggestions and tests them by actually living with them. Such a philosophy, he would maintain, is scientific, but not in the Hegelian sense that it takes shape as a complete system. That rather is scientific which seeks truth by bold experiments.

This principle of the affirmation of life provided him with a criterion to be applied to the history of culture. He employs it especially in *The Birth of Tragedy*, where he distinguishes two tendencies within Greek culture, attaching to one the name of Dionysus and to the other that of Apollo. He was so brilliant a classical scholar that he was appointed to a chair at Basle before he had qualified for it by taking his doctor's degree, and this book was the first fruits of his scholarship. It was dismissed at the time as a work of imagination rather than of erudition, but its main contention is widely accepted today. The two elements he detects resemble closely those Jaspers has called 'the law of the day' and 'the passion of the night'. One is the Dionysian urge, dynamic, creative, ecstatic, frenzied even at times; the other is the Apollonian order, reason, and discipline. The triumph of Greek art was in a synthesis of the two. The Olympian gods attained their calm and serenity by the sublimation of darker and more elemental forces.

> The intricate relation of the Apollonian and the Dionysian in tragedy must really be symbolized by a fraternal union of the two deities: Dionysus speaks the language of Apollo: Apollo, however, finally speaks the language of Dionysus; and so the highest goal of tragedy and of art in general is attained.[2]

In his later work, the relation between the two changes. There is no longer an attempt to keep the balance; Dionysus is allowed to absorb Apollo. In this new form he becomes a symbol for the affirmation of life in face of the harshest circumstances, while Apollo comes to stand for the flight from life into a realm of ideals that is therefore one of illusions. He speaks now of 'Dionysian pessimism', the tragic attitude to

[2] *The Birth of Tragedy*, in *Works*, English translation, p. 167.

life that scorns any wish that things were other than they are, the attitude of the hero who is so strong and self-reliant that he welcomes the buffetings of life and would go to seek them if they did not come to him. The Dionysian, he writes in the appendix to the same book, is

> a formula of *highest affirmation*, born of fullness and overfullness, a yea-saying without reserve to suffering's self, to guilt's self, to all that is questionable and strange in existence itself.[3]

Nietzsche turns again and again to this idea of a form of life that is so rich, joyous, and strong that it finds an opportunity for self-expression even in the most adverse circumstances. And, however one may quarrel with the use to which he puts it, one cannot well deny its nobility.

It is this saying 'Yes' to life that lies behind an element in Nietzsche's thought that some interpreters find difficult to reconcile with the rest of his teaching. It is the Eternal Recurrence, according to which all things come round again and again, so that what is happening now has happened many times already and will happen many times again. Is not this sheer fatalism? What room does it leave for freedom? But we have not reckoned with the exuberant vitality of Dionysian man. He demonstrates his freedom by taking up into his will this whole state of things and proudly affirming it. Standing in the present he says to what threatens him with a repetition of his suffering: "Come again and again, I will to meet you a thousand times more, and each time to conquer you". The Eternal Recurrence makes possible the maximum affirmation of life.

> Oh! how should I not burn for Eternity, and for the marriage ring of rings—the Ring of Recurrence?
> Never yet found I the woman by whom I would have children, save it be by this Woman that I love: for I love thee, O Eternity.
> For I love thee, O Eternity![4]

[3] *Ibid.,* p. 192.
[4] *Thus Spake Zarathustra,* Everyman's Library, p. 206.

CHAPTER III   The Death of God

NIETZSCHE therefore bids us affirm life, and affirm it most where it is most threatened. But what is the catastrophe that hangs over us, the dire threat that is all the more menacing because so few are aware of it? He describes it in the most powerful of his parables.

Have you ever heard of the madman who on a bright morning lighted a lantern and ran to the market-place calling out unceasingly: 'I seek God! I seek God!' As there were many people standing about who did not believe in God, he caused a great deal of amusement. . . . The insane man jumped into their midst and transfixed them with his glances. 'Where is God gone?' he called out. 'I mean to tell you! We have killed him—you and I! We are all his murderers! But how have we done it? How were we able to drink up the sea? Who gave us the sponge to wipe away the whole horizon? What did we do when we loosened this earth from the sun? Whither does it now move? Whither do we move? . . . Is there still an above and below? Do we not stray, as through infinite nothingness? Does not empty space breathe upon us? . . . God is dead! God remains dead! And we have killed him! How shall we console ourselves, the most murderous of all murderers? The holiest and the mightiest that the world has hitherto possessed, has bled to death under our knife —who will wipe the blood from us? . . . There never was a greater event—and on account of it, all who are born after us belong to a higher history than any history hitherto!' [5]

God is dead. Men have killed him. But they do not realize what they have done. The parable continues:

This prodigious event is still on its way, and is travelling—it has not yet reached men's ears.

[5] *The Joyful Wisdom*, pp. 167f.

What is meant by the 'death of God'? It means that human life no longer has an eternal background, is no longer undergirded by a wisdom beyond its own and directed by standards that claim absolute allegiance. This has come about almost by accident, and those who are responsible for the change do not yet grasp what has happened. The supernatural has gone because there was no longer any place for it. It is compatible neither with modern knowledge nor with the modern style of life. To be sure, men continue to bow to it in respect as though there were still something in the place that has been left empty by its departure. They are not yet aware of the frightful hazards to which they are exposed, now that they have been deprived of the old security. What stares us in the face is—just nothing! Nihilism menaces us.

The old values have lost their force. But man cannot live without values. Nietzsche is not an amoralist; he is passionately concerned that there should be direction and standards. But nothing beyond man is now available to give him these. He must therefore give them to himself. Nietzsche, as we have said, knew himself called to a mission. We now see what the mission is. It is the 'transvaluation of values'. To be sure, his work is largely negative; for men have first to be convinced that the old values are worthless before they will consider new ones. He presents himself to his time as a new Zarathustra, and that for two reasons. In the first place, since the Persian prophet was emphatically a moral teacher, one of the makers of the old tables of good and bad, he is aptly depicted as foreswearing that error. In the second place, he put truthfulness at the head of the virtues, and it is through truthfulness that morality is now to be surpassed.

The overcoming of morality through itself—through truthfulness, the overcoming of the moralist through his opposite—*through me*—that is what the name Zarathustra means in my mouth.[6]

By 'morality' Nietzsche means, of course, the traditional Christian morality of Western Europe. This he repudiates, not in the interest of self-indulgence, but

[6] *Thus Spake Zarathustra*, in *Works*, p. xxvi.

that he may reach a standard for conduct that is founded upon truth. Where then is this to be sought? It is customary to divide his development into three periods. In the first, he was under the influence of Schopenhauer and Wagner; in the second science attracted him; and in the third he came into possession of his own distinctive message. For Schopenhauer, the world is the product of Will, a blind will that attains to consciousness in man. Man sees how pain outweighs happiness in a world so fashioned and looks on suffering with pity.[7] Wagner's music owed much to this metaphysic of the will and the ethic derived from it. Though Nietzsche eventually broke with both his mentors, he retained the concept of Will. And the reading of Darwin reinforced this. For did not Darwin present the struggle for existence, in other words the Will to Live, as the driving force behind the evolutionary process? And was not Nietzsche concerned to affirm Life and therefore the Will to Live?

Yes, but not merely the will to exist. That is as abhorrent to him as Schopenhauer's negative attitude to life, recommending escape from it by aesthetic contemplation and ascetic practices. Life is vitality, self-assertion, power. There we have what is wanted. Nietzsche comes forward with a new morality based on the Will to Power. This does not mean that we can decide what is good by asking what is conducive to power. It means that the man of powerful soul and body, the man full of life and resolved to affirm life, will have within himself the criterion of what is noble or base. Nietzsche prefers this antithesis to that of good and bad. There is to be a return to Greek culture as it was before the rationalism of Socrates vitiated it, to the virtues of an aristocracy that does not conceal its contempt for the many and needs no law but its own inherent nobility. Such a human type exists among us already in a few rare individuals; the task for the future is to produce it. The Will to Power aspires beyond man to Superman, in whom alone it will be fulfilled.

[7] Cf. Thomas Hardy: *The Dynasts.*

CHAPTER IV

The Will to Power

As Nietzsche sees it, the Will to Power is the source at once of what is and of what ought to be. As the former, it comes to expression even in the morality he discards. The weaker characters composing the herd are unable, because of their weakness, to affirm life; they accordingly construct a morality that will enable them to evade it and yet withal to gain power. They do this when they sanctify their own weakness by preaching the virtues of pity, love of the neighbour, and so on, while branding as evil such things as "voluptuousness, power of passion, and selfishness." They are incapable of these, and they stand to suffer at the hands of the strong who dare to practice them; they therefore fetter the noble and the healthy with their prohibitions. Christianity, Democracy, and Socialism are so many examples of this 'herd morality'. Democracy pretends that all men are equal and obliterates the distinction between the noble and the base; Socialism would abolish the leisure class that is the mainstay of culture and cater instead for the taste of the mass. Yet all such systems are at bottom only forms of indirect satisfaction for the Will to Power. He who cannot raise himself to the level of those above him can at any rate drag them down to his in the name of brotherhood.

Nietzsche's keen psychological insight is not to be questioned. He has uncovered the rationalizations with which psychoanalysis has made us all too familiar, and the followers of Adler operate with the Will to Power as one of the basic impulses in the human self. He has exposed the ideologies with which groups operate when they seek their own interests. Marx has done as much for all groups except his own; the proletariat has no axe to grind. Nietzsche bids us not be deceived; we have only to listen and the whirr of the whetstone will betray the Communist's secret. He carries the analysis still further by what he has to say of *resentment*. Resentment is the envy of the commonplace for the noble, the impulse to destroy or defame those whose qualities show up one's ugly defects. It is the weapon of the mean and base, and they will never admit that they resort to it. Marx interpreted history in terms of class-struggle; Nietzsche would interpret class-struggle by psychological factors. We must allow for the personal resentment of Marx because he was excluded from the academic career he coveted, and the mass-resentment of the workers against those who flaunt their wealth. And when Communism threatens, Fascism organizes against it the resentment particularly of the lower middle class. But in the noble soul there is no resentment; there the Will to Power is overt and acknowledged, frank and sincere.

We now understand what is meant by 'transvaluation of values'. The currency of moral judgment is to be melted down and minted into a fresh set of coins. What has been condemned for centuries is now to be applauded, and *vice versa*. But there is no suggestion here that all restraint may be thrown off. In the opening parable of *Thus Spake Zarathustra*, Nietzsche makes it clear that his call is to arduous self-discipline and not to laxity. He symbolizes this by the three figures of camel, lion, and child. Man must begin, that is to say, by the acceptance of a rule imposed upon him from without; only so can he become free and reach the stage at which he can defy with his 'I will' the dragon that confronts him with 'Thou shalt'. But the final stage is not this self-conscious assertion: it is a new naturalness and spontaneity, to accept and live out one's life in simplicity and directness. We need not agree with Nietzsche that such a transvaluation of values is called for; we must at least do him the justice to appreciate what it is he seeks to do.

It is here we come to the crucial difficulty in any exposition of Nietzsche. Historically, he has been acclaimed by Fascism and National Socialism, and his books were certainly favourite reading with Mussolini. Even in 1914, there were those who denounced him as the evil genius behind German militarism. A more recent tendency is to acquit him on all these charges, to maintain that he has been grossly misunderstood, and to blame his sister, Frau Förster-Nietzsche, for the 'Nietzsche legend' she put into circulation. Take, for example, the notorious passage in *Thus Spake Zarathustra*.

Ye shall love peace as a means to new wars—and short peace better than long. . . .

Do ye say that a good cause halloweth even war? I say to you; a good war halloweth any cause.

War and courage have done greater things than charity.[8]

We know enough of Nietzsche's reaction to his short service in the Franco-German war to doubt whether this language is to be taken literally. In the same passage he says:

I see many soldiers: would I saw many warriors! 'Uniform' are their garments called: would that were not uniform they conceal beneath!

It seems best to treat all this as poetry and symbolism. He seeks "warriors of knowledge", to use his own words. What he has in mind is the spiritual combat in which a man overcomes himself, subdues the chaos in him to a star.

It is to be regretted that he used language so inclined to mislead. His ideal is clearly an aristocratic one. It is realized in the man who raises himself above his fellows by his powers of body and mind, making no apology for his intrinsic superiority but boldly living it out. He will be hard, pitiless, and stern with himself and others, since these are the health-giving qualities. He will possess 'the bestowing virtue', the superfluity that cannot be contained within the one who possesses it, but must pour itself out. Even Nietzsche's praise of selfishness is no approval of the self-centred and the niggardly.

Then is your body exalted and raised up; its bliss raviseth the spirit so that it becometh a creator and a valuer and a lover and a benefactor of all things.[9]

8 *Ibid.*, Everyman's Library, p. 39.
9 *Ibid.*, p. 67.

CHAPTER V   The Superman

SOMETHING has already been said of the influence on Nietzsche of science in general and of Darwin in particular. The evolutionary hypothesis could not fail to attract the attention of one concerned, as Nietzsche was, with what it means to be human. For, at first sight, Darwin appeared to threaten man with wholesale degradation, with reduction to the ranks of the beast. Was he more than a higher specimen of animal? What would happen once this knowledge had spread among the masses? Might not a new and more terrifying barbarism be the result? Yet once again, only he who is willing to accept the menace is in a position to overcome it. Looked at from one point of view, Darwinism did mean that man was only a more highly-developed animal. Yet from another point of view it opened out a prospect of further development that would surpass man and bring the Superman. In the final phase of his work, Nietzsche therefore came forward as prophet of the Superman.

> The Superman is the meaning of the earth. Let your will say: the Superman *shall be* the meaning of the earth. . . .
> Man is a rope stretched between beast and Superman—a rope over an abyss. . . .
> Man is great in that he is a bridge and not a goal: man can be loved in that he is a transition and not a perishing.[10]

What is meant by the Superman? There is no suggestion that any *existing* human group is biologically superior to others or destined to act as a master-race.[11] For the Germans Nietzsche had nothing but contempt and liked to think of himself as of Polish descent. He could express warm admiration for the Jews and one

[10] *Ibid.*, pp. 6f.
[11] Nietzsche does indeed imply at one point that terms like 'good' and 'bad' may have been connected *originally* with racial differences. *Genealogy of Morals*, pp. 22f.

reason for his objection to his sister's marriage with Herr Förster was that the latter was an avowed anti-Semite. He described the state as the 'cold monster', crushing all true human worth underfoot; he dreaded its ever-increasing and ever-encroaching powers, whether exercised by a Bismarck or by Social Democracy. His ideal was the good European and he professed himself to be such. He wanted to end the hectic and stupid nationalisms that plagued the Continent with wars and to substitute for them a unifying culture.

A thousand goals have there been heretofore, for there have been a thousand peoples. But the yoke upon the thousand necks is lacking, the one goal is lacking. Mankind hath as yet no goal.

But tell me, I pray, my brethren: if a goal be lacking to mankind, is not mankind itself lacking?[12]

But there is no excuse for the language Nietzsche at times permitted himself to use. He could speak of the common people as the dung that must be spread thick so that a single flower may grow. The Superman is the being who will come as man learns to transcend himself. Clearly, only the noble, only those in whom the Will to Power is exceptionally strong, will aspire beyond themselves in this way. The higher man who is more than man will be the aristocrat, a centre of radiant and bestowing virtue; he will be a law to himself, whether to create or to enjoy. He will be the Dionysian of the new type described at this period; the figure of abounding vitality, surging powers, and exuberant self-expression who will yet bring all these into harmony. "I say unto you: a man must have chaos yet within him to give birth to a dancing star." [13] He will be the strong, alert, self-confident but self-disciplined individual, self-creating and lifted high above the nameless multitude who have worth only as they admire and serve him. Such an ideal is the stark antithesis of that of Marx, for whom the 'coming race' is the proletariat, now despised but then triumphant. It is equally opposed to Kierkegaard's "individual before God", who never claims to be more than what every man has it in him to become.

[12] *Thus Spake Zarathustra*, p. 51.
[13] *Ibid.*, p. 9.

The Superman is a product of 'breeding', no doubt. But in what sense? There certainly are passages in which Nietzsche seems to advocate eugenics and it is difficult to dismiss these as rhetoric, especially in view of his own ill health and his affirmation of life over against this. Yet in *Ecce Homo* he stigmatizes as "learned cattle" those who so understand him.[14] If we are to take the reference to 'breeding' metaphorically, it will be training that Nietzsche has in mind. Not to be sure formal education of any kind, but rather the cultivation of free, open, bold and daring personalities, the set of the will towards the noble rather than towards the 'good'.

He hath subdued monsters, he hath solved riddles: but he must yet resolve his monsters and his riddles, he must change them to heavenly children.[15]

There are times, however, when the Superman seems to be identified with one or other of the great historical figures, a Caesar Borgia, a Napoleon, a Caesar or a Goethe. Even Socrates was admitted to this select company in the end. The Superman, we may perhaps say, can only be produced in the future because man as such has potentialities waiting to be developed, and some in the past and present have travelled farther than others in this direction. But in none of them is the ideal fully realized, the ideal, that is, of the man who

has overcome his animal nature, organized the chaos of his passions, sublimated his impulses, and given style to his character—or, as Nietzsche said of Goethe: 'he disciplined himself into wholeness, he *created* himself' and became 'the man of tolerance, not from weakness but from strength', 'a spirit who has *become free*'.[16]

[14] *Op. cit.*, p. 58.
[15] *Thus Spake Zarathustra*, p. 108.
[16] Walter A. Kaufmann: *Nietzsche*, 1950, p. 278.

WHAT precedes has already made clear that Nietzsche waged war without truce against Christianity. Others had done this before him; what is distinctive of him is that his quarrel was with the Christian ethic even more than Christian doctrine. The old table of values that was to be replaced by a new one was the Christian table. Nietzsche coined his new commandment in opposition to the old "Thou shalt love thy neighbour as thyself".

> Let things future and farthest be the motive of thy today: in thy friend shalt thou love the Superman as thy motive.
> My brethren, I counsel you not love of the neighbour—I counsel you love of them that are farthest.[17]

It is difficult not to think that resentment was at work in his furious antagonism to Christianity. Could there be anything more revealing than the confession that follows?

> But that I may reveal unto you my whole heart, my friends—if there were gods, how could I endure not to be a god! *Therefore* there are no gods.[18]

Like many others, Nietzsche distinguished between Jesus himself and the religion that arose out of him. He presents Jesus as a rebel against the traditional order within Judaism and so has to some extent engaged in the transvaluation of values. He was condemned because his mission to publicans and sinners and his criticism of the Law threatened to undermine the Will to Power of the Jewish people. He can also describe Jesus—in a passage subsequently altered for publication—as an 'idiot' in the sense in which Dostoievsky used that word for the central figure in one of his novels.[19] That is to say,

[17] *Thus Spake Zarathustra*, p. 53.
[18] *Ibid.*, p. 76.
[19] Kaufmann, *Op. cit.*, p. 298.

Jesus was neither a strong soul nor a weak one; he was childlike and indifferent to suffering. He did not resent evil because he did not feel deeply enough the sting and hurt of it. This is a caricature, no doubt, yet it contains some features of a genuine portrait. Nietzsche has grasped the union of opposites in Jesus, the combination of humility and meekness with scathing condemnation of the representatives of religion and morality. The mercy that received the Magdalene was one with the severity that drove the hucksters from the temple, since their common root was in his mission to act for God.

The severest criticisms were directed against Paul and therefore against Luther. The language at this point becomes so vehement as to suggest the pathological. Paul's boldest and most obnoxious invention was justification by faith. For this Nietzsche has not the slightest understanding. He represents it as a clever device by which those who are intellectually stupid or lack strength of will excuse themselves on the score of few pious emotions. Sick souls as they are, they construct for themselves a tortured God and worship him. Bitter and resentful, they dream of a last judgment and the fires of an eternal hell for those who do not 'believe', that is, have the hardihood to differ from them. The morality that issues from such a set of doctrines is a crime against life; it was devised as a means by which the submerged masses of the ancient world could take a mean revenge on all that was noble and masterful.

Nothing is to be gained by going into further details. The crucial point is that for Nietzsche Christian morality is a morality of weakness, whereas he can accept no morality that is not based on, and an expression of, strength. He detects the 'Christian poison' even in what others describe as 'materialist Socialism'. For it too is the revenge the weak take upon the strong. And resentment and revenge are incompatible with the affirmation of life. What is the Christian reply to these accusations? In my judgment, it is necessary to take them seriously and to admit that sometimes the thrust finds its way home. Is it not sometimes the case that what purports to be forgiveness is not an act of strength, in which the injury done is felt deeply and judged inflexibly yet not allowed to bar the wrongdoer's return to fellowship, but one of weakness, in which what happened is not taken seriously. Where does the Christian pacifist stand, for example? Is his refusal an evasion of conflict out of timidity or fear, or is it the choice of a sterner struggle on the spiritual plane?

The love of the neighbour can be perverted into concern for those only within one's narrow circle. When this happens, it needs to be broken into by a love that ranges farther afield and cares for future generations and for distant lands. But did not Jesus say that he came to give abundant life? Is he not presented in the Fourth Gospel as the life of men? Cannot such language be taken as accepting Nietzsche's affirmation of life and raising it to a higher level? I do not see why the Christian ideal should not make room for the passionate man who subdues his passions to style and order, though it will always affirm that self-realization comes by surrender to what lies beyond the self. In so many words, the study of Nietzsche ought to have a tonic effect on the Christian, enabling him to distinguish the genuine from the spurious in such virtues as pity, humility, and unselfishness by asking whether they are in a particular case the expression of strength or of weakness.

Marx and Nietzsche—we conclude with these two our broad survey of Western thought. They represent respectively the subordination of the individual to the class and the subjection of the mass to the individual. We can be content with neither. For events have taught us that there is a secret alliance between them; the mass-movement and the tyrant call for each other. Our task is to create a society in which persons will come into their own, in which the man of outstanding ability will not provoke resentment and the common man will not be an object of contempt. Did not the Christian love that both Marx and Nietzsche despised aim at something of this order?

For further reading:

Translations of Nietzsche's works.
J. Lavrin: *Friedrich Nietzsche An Approach.*
F. Copleston: *Friedrich Nietzsche.*
W. A. Kaufmann: *Nietzsche.*

Appendix

THE temptation to prolong into the present the story that has hitherto been confined to the past is a powerful one and the reader would perhaps not have it resisted. The trouble is, of course, that what is wanted is not so much a judgment on the present as a window open upon the future. There is a large measure of agreement on the influences that have shaped the world in which we live; those that will set their stamp upon the future it is difficult to discern. They will not necessarily be those that attract most attention just now. Indeed, as far as ideas are concerned—and it is these that form our theme—it would seem that uncertainty is characteristic of our time, and that none can tell which of the conflicting trends of thought will in the end prevail.

For example, science, both pure and applied, is a factor of increasing importance, and one prophecy that may be safely ventured is that its power will not decrease. The conflict between science and religion has largely abated, and the present discussion seems to turn mainly on the limits of science. We are back, that is to say, where Kant stood, only now the science with which we operate is at once more far-reaching and more modest than that with which he was familiar. It has given us an imposing body of knowledge, but it has abandoned the claim to put at our disposal a final truth. Its laws are statistical, dealing with probabilities rather than certainties, and there are instances in which it cannot decide between two alternative formulations; its assertions, we are told, are valid rather than true; they are like the contour lines on a map, which do not at all reproduce the features of the landscape but all the same are invaluable as guides to the traveller. But if the natural sciences in this way lose their rigidity and finality, they draw all the nearer on that account to the social sciences, where experiment is out of the question and prediction hazardous. The old claim that social problems would gain immensely by the application of scientific method therefore comes back, and indeed its validity is assumed in much of our legislation and administration. But what are the limits to this procedure? At what point does the scientific organization of society pass over into the dreaded dehumanization of man? These are the questions with which we are exercised today.

In current philosophy there are two opposed tendencies, one dominant on the Continent and the other in Britain. The latter is known by various names, *logical analysis* being perhaps as appropriate as any. It is concerned with the nature of language and with the treatment of philosophical problems from the angle of linguistic usage. We may say that while Kant asked what we can hope to know, the new school points out that language is an essential tool of knowledge, and that we need to take time to consider just what can and can not be done with it. There was at one time an easy assumption that this procedure would enable us, not so much to solve the great problems as to dismiss them.

> The cloud of mortal destiny,
> Others may front it fearlessly,
> But who, like him, will put it by?

It was then supposed that the statements of natural science are the standard to which all other statements about our experience must conform on pain of being relegated to the class of tautologies or dismissed as meaningless. There is now a readiness to admit that ethical and aesthetic, religious and metaphysical statements have a right to be considered on their respective merits. There are different levels of language, each with its appropriate usage and standards.

The other tendency in philosophy is the *existentialist,* which stems from Kierkegaard. The system-building ambition of a Hegel is as remote from the existentialists as from the logical analysts, though for a different reason. They have learned from Kierkegaard that life often mocks at logic and their attention is drawn precisely to those experiences that are too profound and personal for ordinary language to do justice to them. They call us back to the wonder that is at the root of all philosophizing, they bid us make our inescapable mortality the theme of reflection, and they enlarge our concept of truth so that it includes what transforms our being as well as what extends our information. To be sure, they do not all speak with one voice. If Sartre declares man to be but a "useless passion", an ever-renewed and ever-defeated effort to be as God, Marcel offers us a metaphysic of hope. If Heidegger borrows the language of Christian theology for his analysis of what it means to "be-in-the-world", Jaspers echoes the Biblical message in a terminology of his own.

In Protestant theology, a similar situation of conflict obtains. On the one hand, there is a return to the Reformation and even, in the case of Karl Barth, to the scholasticism of the seventeenth century; on the other, there is a resolute attempt, with which the name of Rudolf Bultmann is associated, to come to grips with the world of applied science into which our generation is born. If the one wishes to ensure that the Christian faith is retained intact and not compromised by any dealings with the spirit of the times, the other is concerned that the man of today shall be challenged by the Christian gospel and not be put off from any reckoning with it because of the strange form in which it is presented to him. A religion, it is clear, can only have power as it is at once faithful to its distinctive mission and relevant to the situation to which it speaks. The question is how these two demands can be met at the same time. Or must one always be sacrificed to the other?

All this, of course, is tentative in the extreme. Can nothing be said that is more certain? In the preceding pages the effort has been made to follow the development of Western thought from its origins in Greece, Rome, and Jerusalem. We have seen the influence upon it of crucial events and outstanding personalities, but there has been little evidence of any contact with what was taking place in other centres of civilization. Even within Europe it was possible to confine our attention to what was happening west of the great Russian landmass. Such an isolation of the West will be impossible in the future. The time has come for Europe to take seriously both the Russian and the Asian contributions to what must become a common stock. Already, exiles from the East European countries have introduced us to a thought-world, rich and strange, from which we must be willing to learn. The Christianity of Byzantium must be incorporated into our heritage along with that of Rome. The effect of India and China upon us is likely to be even greater.

This is not the place in which to tell how Europe first became aware, through pilgrims, missionaries, and crusaders, of Islam, a faith so like its own and yet so hostile to it that Christians suspected that diabolical influences were at work in it. Jesuit missions surprised the intelligentsia at home with their reports of Chinese culture. European scholars learned Sanskrit and made Indian speculation known. But it was not until the twentieth century that some knowledge of Asian philosophy and religion became an essential part of the equipment of an educated person in the West. We are now aware that no one continent has a monopoly of wisdom, and only our unhappy political divisions hold back an interchange of ideas on a world-scale. The next task of the Western mind is to cease to be merely Western and to join with the Eastern mind, whether in Europe or beyond it, in that unreserved communication by which alone a common truth can be won.

INDEX